MOLIÈRE

# Tartuffe

TRANSLATED AND EDITED BY
## Haskell M. Block
BROOKLYN COLLEGE

APPLETON-CENTURY-CROFTS, Inc.
*New York*

PRINTED IN THE UNITED STATES OF AMERICA
E-23103

# TARTUFFE

where the audience's interest was enhanced by the
censorship of the play, and he presented private performances of the comedy before nobility at their country estates, quite possibly with the king's tacit approval. Not only did Molière need the comedy for his
repertoire, but, as contemporary evidence makes clear,
he was fully convinced that it would be a tremendous
financial success, and subsequent events were to prove
him correct. Above all, there is no doubt that the
temporary victory of "the Tartuffes," in which "the
models have succeeded in eliminating the copy," only
buttressed Molière's tenacity.

In 1667 he was ready to try again. The *Second Petition* to the king, written on August 6 of that year,
tells the story of his failure. In vain did Molière soften
his religious satire, rename his central figure Panulphe,
and eliminate all priestly resemblance. Before a second performance could take place, the director of
administration and police had banned the play, and
this blow was followed by an edict of the Archbishop
of Paris forbidding all persons in his diocese to perform, read, or hear recited this "very dangerous" play
under pain of excommunication. The edict was sub-
sequently set aside, but the prohibition was enough
to discourage Molière and drive him to the brink of
desperation: "It is certain, Sire," he wrote to the king
who was commanding his armies in Flanders, "that I
need not think of writing comedies if the Tartuffes are
triumphant." The king gave his assurances, and Molière bided his time. On February 5, 1669, well after
the turmoil of public controversy had subsided, Louis
XIV granted his personal authorization for the performance of the play. Four days later *Tartuffe* was
presented in public in the version that we read and
see today.

In approaching Molière's play it is important to remember that he lived with it and worked on it for
almost five years. He found time in the meanwhile to

write nine other plays, some of which are among his very best, but from 1664 to 1669 the composition of *Tartuffe* proceeded through three versions, and there can be no doubt that the demands of revision have left their mark upon the final text. In all likelihood, the version of 1669 represents a considerable hardening and sharpening of the play's satiric force. The *Preface* which Molière wrote in March of 1669 when the play was first printed, is at once a justification of his comedy and a celebration of its triumph. More important, it is one of the most vigorous assertions of the artist's right to freedom of expression that we can find anywhere in literature. The reader should bear in mind that the *Preface* was penned later than all of the *Petitions* to the king; it is a clear and incisive statement of Molière's dramatic theory as well as a spirited defense of *Tartuffe,* projecting in bold relief the moral and satiric values of Molière's art.

Nevertheless, we should not forget, as Molière himself asserts, that there is a wide difference between a direct moral or philosophical statement and a drama; and Molière's characters and situations speak to us in a language far more immediate and alive than that of any tract or discussion. In its simplest elements the play is a series of comic scenes in which a rogue practices deception on his dupe, to his own advantage and to the detriment of the dupe and his dependents. In essence, both Tartuffe and Orgon emerge out of stock types in which the character's identity is his mask, and to this extent, typical and representative values are always present. Even the name of Tartuffe is significant; it derives from *truffe* or deception, and *tartuffe* was employed in French in the fifteenth and sixteenth centuries as an epithet addressed to crooks and cheats. The dramatic action consists of alternations between pretense and reality, and the principal movement of the play is the process of identifying and unmasking the central character.

Tartuffe is a far more subtle creation than the wooden figures of French or Italian farce. Well before he makes his appearance in Act III, we know something of his cleverness and guile; the pretense of piety and asceticism is an essential part of the hypocrite's mask. Tartuffe's very first words in the play proclaim the mortification of the flesh, but we know from earlier accounts how much he relishes good food and drink, as well as other physical comforts. It was a master stroke on the part of his creator to make him sensual as well as cunning, for it is his own weakness rather than chance, skill, or the mere assertion of truth which precipitates his downfall. Some readers feel that Tartuffe is stupid beyond belief in allowing Elmire to dupe him so easily, but his behavior provides all the more convincing proof that his artifice is surpassed by his sensuality. In our traditional sympathy with the underdog, we may sometimes wonder if Tartuffe rather than Orgon is not the victim, if he is not more honest and sincere than those who oppose him. The problem is complicated by the fact that when Tartuffe exposes himself to Elmire or damns himself out before Orgon, he brazenly drops his mask and stands before us in his essential reality. It would certainly be wrong to view Tartuffe as a monster, but he is undoubtedly a dangerous crook. Like criminals of every time and place, he overreaches himself, but his final defeat is far more fortuitous than the strictest canons of dramatic probability might admit.

The conclusion of the play has been warmly admired by actors for its marvellous theatrical effectiveness, but our knowledge of the history of *Tartuffe* from 1664 to 1669 should explain in large part why Molière so abundantly praised the magnanimity of *le roi soleil*. Certainly if Louis XIV had not approved of the attitudes or enjoyed the comedy in the play, he would not have supported Molière as he did. The conclusion is a fitting tribute to an enlightened monarch.

Molière could have ended his play in other ways, for, according to the laws of the time, Orgon's donation was legally void: a man could not give away all of his property even if he wanted to, and donations could always be revoked at the donor's pleasure. Unquestionably, the ending Molière chose makes for more effective theater, for it carries Tartuffe to the very brink of absolute success, and no conclusion could be more dramatic than the reversal which comes in the very moment of his apparent triumph.

It would be well here and throughout not to view the play according to the canons of present-day realism. It is as futile to attempt to identify the supposed model of Molière's scoundrel as it is to read the comedy as a latter-day "problem play." Bottles of ink have been wasted in these pursuits. *Tartuffe* is a play, not a tract, and while it is wrong to contend, as do some recent interpreters, that Molière was largely unconcerned with moral and religious values, our interest is aroused primarily by the way in which these are made a part of Molière's art. Thus, while the play is often cited as evidence of Molière's views on the importance of rationality and moderation, Cléante, the *raisonneur* of the piece, plays virtually no part in the action; the dramatic experience of the comedy and its dynamic movement stem from the unreasonable and irrational qualities of Orgon's character.

Orgon is indeed as unrealistic a figure as can be found anywhere in drama, yet by means of the exposition of Act I, his behavior is made sufficiently credible for the sake of the action that follows. If Orgon's conduct is outlandish, at least it is consistently so, and if we remember that he is the son of Madame Pernelle and father of Damis, we can all the more readily accept rashness and excitability as among his essential traits. From his first appearance we are amused and delighted by his folly, but we know too that he was once a good man who has only recently turned fool and easy dupe. As such, he is fair game; his actions toward his family effectively insulate him from any sympathy on the part of the audience, and his stupidity is a constant source of the keenest exhilaration. If Orgon is genuinely funny, he is also, in moments of the play, ugly and dangerous: "I do not want to be liked," he tells Dorine, and under Tartuffe's guidance he becomes a menace not only to himself but to all around him. He would compel his daughter to marry against her will; he disinherits and banishes his son, and throws his wife into the arms of her seducer. He is a bad husband, a bad father, and a bad citizen, and he must be manipulated, not simply to learn the truth about Tartuffe, but for the common good. Orgon's abdication of his reason leads to a complete breakdown in social relationships, yet without this abdication there would be no comedy.

The action of the play is incomparable in its simplicity and verve. Goethe, himself a master of dramatic technique, called the exposition of *Tartuffe* the finest in the whole of dramatic literature, of compelling significance and theatrical interest in itself, yet giving rise to tremendous consequences. The latter part of Act II may seem unduly episodic, but from the begining of Act III to the very end, the speed and movement of the play is unrelenting. Deception and surprise are inherent in the very fabric of the plot, and, until the final curtain, neither characters nor audience are permitted a moment's complacency or rest. With the keenest insight into passions and motives and with an almost breath-taking economy, Molière exploits the fluid lines between appearance and reality, credulity and knowledge, to the wonder and delight of all who see or read the play. As Voltaire summed it up two hundred years ago, *Tartuffe* will last as long as there are hypocrites and men who know how to enjoy great art.

# A NOTE ON THE TEXT

THE FOLLOWING translation is an attempt to present *Tartuffe* to the American reader in a version that is both accurate and alive. Although Molière wrote his play in alexandrine couplets, the language of present-day prose is much closer to his idiom than that of verse. The translator has been aided at several points by the excellent version of John Ozell of 1714. The text of the present translation follows the edition of René Bray (see *Bibliography*). The editions of Pierre Clarac and H. Ashton, and the acting version of Fernand Ledoux, have been of special help.

# PRINCIPAL DATES IN MOLIÈRE'S LIFE

❧

| | |
|---|---|
| 1622 | Birth of Jean-Baptiste Poquelin (Molière), in Paris on January 15, the eldest son of a prosperous upholsterer. |
| 1639 | Finishes studies at Collège de Clermont, Paris. |
| 1642 | Receives degree from Faculty of Law at Orléans. |
| 1643 | Establishes Illustre Théâtre, Paris, and takes the name of Molière. |
| 1645 | Molière's troupe, bankrupt, leaves Paris for the provinces. |
| 1653 | *L'Étourdi*, first original play, staged in Lyon. |
| 1658 | Molière's troupe returns to Paris. |
| 1659 | *Les Précieuses ridicules*, first successful play. |
| 1662 | Marriage to Armande Béjart, actress. |
| 1662 | *L'École des femmes*. |
| 1663 | Molière receives a pension from Louis XIV, as an indication of court favor. |
| 1664 | First version of *Tartuffe*. |
| 1665 | *Don Juan*. |
| 1665 | Molière's troupe named "The King's Company" by Louis XIV. |

1666    *Le Misanthrope.*

1666    *Le Médecin malgré lui.*

1667    Second version of *Tartuffe,* banned after one performance.

1668    *Amphitryon.*

1668    *L'Avare.*

1669    Final version of *Tartuffe.*

1670    *Le Bourgeois gentilhomme.*

1672    *Les Femmes savantes.*

1673    *Le Malade imaginaire.*

1673    Death of Molière, on February 17, at the close of the fourth performance of *Le Malade imaginaire.*

# INTRODUCTION

At a distance of three centuries Molière's great comedies are so rich and vital a part of our dramatic heritage that they have come to exemplify a kind of perfection in their art, unrivalled anywhere in world drama. To read or to see a comedy of Molière is to enter in some measure into the dynamics of his artistry, to sense the matchless skill and keen insight into human nature with which he re-created life on the stage. Of all the playwrights of his age and perhaps of any age, he was the most identified with the theater, and when we read his work, we should attempt to envision it as dramatic representation, as a configuration of animated speech and gesture taking shape and body before our eyes.

Molière spent his life on the boards, and his plays cannot be divorced from their theatrical milieu. Writing plays was for Molière but one of many occupations. As an actor he had traveled with his company for over twelve years in the provinces of France; he had carefully observed the Italian players of the *commedia dell' arte* and had learned their art of mask and mime and their techniques of improvisation. He was a skillful performer, but as head of his company he was much more: he managed the troupe, recruited its members, assigned parts, supervised rehearsals, designed sets, selected costumes, and managed all of the business affairs. He was manager, producer, director, playwright, publicist, and actor all combined into one. No wonder that he died at 51! The marvel of it all is that he was able to do so much. Within a period of fourteen years Molière wrote 33 plays. Such rapidity of composition does not make for originality of plot, but in energy of movement and vigor of character revelation, Molière made what he borrowed his own. His best plays—with *Tartuffe* perhaps at their head—impart such life and warmth to audiences everywhere that they have made his name virtually synonymous with comic genius. So sure is Molière's command of character and scene that his art seems far more the product of instinct and chance than of skill and strategy; yet when we examine this art with care and understanding, we can see how directly Molière's knowledge of the theater's ways and means contributed to his achievement.

*Tartuffe* offers an impressive example of Molière's sustained dedication in the pursuit of his art. It was first presented as a three-act play, probably in complete form, on May, 12, 1664 before King Louis XIV and his guests at Versailles. The king seems to have enjoyed the play, but others did not, and three months later Molière was compelled to address his *First Petition* to his monarch. Powerful religious groups exerted great influence at court, and it is very possible that Louis XIV was subjected to pressure from his mother as well as from the Archbishop of Paris to ban Molière's comedy. The chronicles of the day tell us that *Tartuffe* was condemned and banned as a work "absolutely harmful to religion and capable of producing very dangerous effects." The king apparently thought otherwise, for in private he seems to have exonerated Molière of any malicious intent in writing the play; however, in public the monarch was less outspoken, and despite Molière's plaintive appeal in his *First Petition* to the king, the prohibition was not removed.

A lesser writer might have been content to let the matter rest, but Molière redoubled his efforts to gain acceptance of his play. He gave private readings before the most cultivated salons of Parisian society,

# TARTUFFE

## PREFACE

HERE IS A COMEDY that has excited a good deal of discussion and that has been under attack for a long time; and the persons who are mocked by it have made it plain that they are more powerful in France than all whom my plays have satirized up to this time. Noblemen, ladies of fashion, cuckolds, and doctors all kindly consented to their presentation, which they themselves seemed to enjoy along with everyone else; but hypocrites do not understand banter: they became angry at once, and found it strange that I was bold enough to represent their actions and to care to describe a profession shared by so many good men. This is a crime for which they cannot forgive me, and they have taken up arms against my comedy in a terrible rage. They were careful not to attack it at the point that had wounded them: they are too crafty for that and too clever to reveal their true character. In keeping with their lofty custom, they have used the cause of God to mask their private interests; and *Tartuffe*, they say, is a play that offends piety: it is filled with abominations from beginning to end, and nowhere is there a line that does not deserve to be burned. Every syllable is wicked, the very gestures are criminal, and the slightest glance, turn of the head, or step from right to left conceals mysteries that they are able to explain to my disadvantage. In vain did I submit the play to the criticism of my friends and the scrutiny of the public: all the corrections I could make, the judgment of the king and queen who saw

1

the play, the approval of great princes and ministers of state who honored it with their presence, the opinion of good men who found it worthwhile, all this did not help. They will not let go of their prey, and every day of the week they have pious zealots abusing me in public and damning me out of charity.

I would care very little about all they might say except that their devices make enemies of men whom I respect and gain the support of genuinely good men, whose faith they know and who, because of the warmth of their piety, readily accept the impressions that others present to them. And it is this which forces me to defend myself. Especially to the truly devout do I wish to vindicate my play, and I beg of them with all my heart not to condemn it before seeing it, to rid themselves of preconceptions, and not aid the cause of men dishonored by their actions.

If one takes the trouble to examine my comedy in good faith, he will surely see that my intentions are innocent throughout, and tend in no way to make fun of what men revere; that I have presented the subject with all the precautions that its delicacy imposes; and that I have used all the art and skill that I could to distinguish clearly the character of the hypocrite from that of the truly devout man. For that purpose I used two whole acts to prepare the appearance of my scoundrel. Never is there a moment's doubt about his character; he is known at once from the qualities I have given him; and from one end of the play to the other, he does not say a word, he does not perform an action which does not depict to the audience the character of a wicked man, and which does not bring out in sharp relief the character of the truly good man which I oppose to it.

I know full well that by way of reply, these gentlemen try to insinuate that it is not the role of the theater to speak of these matters; but with their permission, I ask them on what do they base this fine doctrine. It is a proposition they advance as no more than a supposition, for which they offer not a shred of proof; and surely it would not be difficult to show them that comedy, for the ancients, had its origin in religion and constituted a part of its ceremonies; that our neighbors, the Spaniards, have hardly a single holiday celebration in which a comedy is not a part; and that even here in France, it owes its birth to the efforts of a religious brotherhood who still own the Hotel de Bourgogne, where the most important mystery plays of our faith were presented; that you can still find comedies printed in gothic letters under the name of a learned doctor of the Sorbonne; and without going so far, in our own day the religious dramas of Pierre Corneille have been performed to the admiration of all France.

If the function of comedy is to correct men's vices, I do not see why any should be exempt. Such a condition in our society would be much more dangerous than the thing itself; and we have seen that the theater is admirably suited to provide correction. The most forceful lines of a serious moral statement are usually less powerful than those of satire; and nothing will reform most men better than the depiction of their faults. It is a vigorous blow to vices to expose them to public laughter. Criticism is taken lightly, but men will not tolerate satire. They are quite willing to be mean, but they never like to be ridiculed.

I have been attacked for having placed words of piety in the mouth of my impostor. Could I avoid doing so in order to represent properly the character of a hypocrite? It seemed to me sufficient to reveal the criminal motives which make him speak as he does, and I have eliminated all ceremonial phrases, which nonetheless he would not have been found using incorrectly. Yet some say that in the fourth act he sets forth a vicious morality; but is not this a morality which everyone has heard again and again?

Does my comedy say anything new here? And is there any fear that ideas so thoroughly detested by everyone can make an impression on men's minds; that I make them dangerous by presenting them in the theater; that they acquire authority from the lips of a scoundrel? There is not the slightest suggestion of any of this; and one must either approve the comedy of *Tartuffe* or condemn all comedies in general.

This has indeed been done in a furious way for some time now, and never was the theater so much abused. I cannot deny that there were Church Fathers who condemned comedy; but neither will it be denied me that there were some who looked on it somewhat more favorably. Thus authority, on which censure is supposed to depend, is destroyed by this disagreement; and the only conclusion that can be drawn from this difference of opinion among men enlightened by the same wisdom is that they viewed comedy in different ways, and that some considered it in its purity, while others regarded it in its corruption and confused it with all those wretched performances which have been rightly called performances of filth.

And in fact, since we should talk about things rather than words, and since most misunderstanding comes from including contrary notions in the same word, we need only to remove the veil of ambiguity and look at comedy in itself to see if it warrants condemnation. It will surely be recognized that as it is nothing more than a clever poem which corrects men's faults by means of agreeable lessons, it cannot be condemned without injustice. And if we listened to the voice of ancient times on this matter, it would tell us that its most famous philosophers have praised comedy—they who professed so austere a wisdom and who ceaselessly denounced the vices of their times. It would tell us that Aristotle spent his evenings at the theater and took the trouble to reduce the art of making comedies to rules. It would tell us that some of its greatest and most honored men took pride in writing comedies themselves; and that others did not disdain to recite them in public; that Greece expressed its admiration for this art by means of handsome prizes and magnificent theaters to honor it; and finally, that in Rome this same art also received extraordinary honors; I do not speak of Rome run riot under the license of the emperors, but of disciplined Rome, governed by the wisdom of the consuls, and in the age of the full vigor of Roman dignity.

I admit that there have been times when comedy became corrupt. And what do men not corrupt every day? There is nothing so innocent that men cannot turn it to crime; nothing so beneficial that its values cannot be reversed; nothing so good in itself that it cannot be put to bad uses. Medical knowledge benefits mankind and is revered as one of our most wonderful possessions; and yet there was a time when it fell into discredit, and was often used to poison men. Philosophy is a gift of Heaven; it has been given to us to bring us to the knowledge of a God by contemplating the wonders of nature; and yet we know that often it has been turned away from its function and has been used openly in support of impiety. Even the holiest of things are not immune from human corruption, and every day we see scoundrels who use and abuse piety, and wickedly make it serve the greatest of crimes. But this does not prevent one from making the necessary distinctions. We do not confuse in the same false inference the goodness of things that are corrupted with the wickedness of the corrupt. The function of an art is always distinguished from its misuse; and as medicine is not forbidden because it was banned in Rome, nor philosophy because it was publicly condemned in Athens, we should not suppress comedy simply because it has been condemned at certain times. This censure was justified then for reasons which no longer apply today; it was limited to what was then seen; and we should not seize on these limits, apply them more rigidly than is necessary, and include in our condemnation the innocent along with the guilty. The comedy that this censure attacked is in no way the comedy that we want to defend. We must be careful not to confuse the one with the other. There may be two persons whose morals may be completely different. They may have no resemblance to one another except in their names, and it would be a terrible injustice to want to condemn Olympia, who is a good woman, because there is also an Olympia who is lewd. Such procedures would make for great confusion everywhere. Everything under the sun would be condemned; now since this rigor is not applied to the countless instances of abuse we see every day, the same should hold for comedy, and those plays should be approved in which instruction and virtue reign supreme.

I know there are some so delicate that they cannot tolerate a comedy, who say that the most decent are the most dangerous, that the passions they present are all the more moving because they are virtuous, and that men's feelings are stirred by these presentations. I do not see what great crime it is to be affected by the sight of a generous passion; and this utter insensitivity to which they would lead us is indeed a high degree of virtue! I wonder if so great a perfection resides within the strength of human nature, and I wonder if it is not better to try to correct and moderate men's passions than to try to suppress them altogether. I grant that there are places better to visit than the theater; and if we want to condemn every single thing that does not bear directly on God and our salvation, it is right that comedy be included, and I should willingly grant that it be condemned along with everything else. But if we admit, as is in fact true, that the exercise of piety will permit interruptions, and that men need amusement, I maintain that there is none more innocent than comedy. I have dwelled too long on this matter. Let me finish with the words of a great prince on the comedy, *Tartuffe*.

Eight days after it had been banned, a play called *Scaramouche the Hermit* was performed before the court; and the king, on his way out, said to this great prince: "I should really like to know why the persons who make so much noise about Molière's comedy do not say a word about *Scaramouche*." To which the prince replied, "It is because the comedy of *Scaramouche* makes fun of Heaven and religion, which these gentlemen do not care about at all, but that of Molière makes fun of *them,* and that is what they cannot bear."

THE AUTHOR

# FIRST PETITION

*(presented to the King on the comedy of Tartuffe)*

Sire,

As the duty of comedy is to correct men by amusing them, I believed that in my occupation I could do nothing better than attack the vices of my age by making them ridiculous; and as hypocrisy is undoubtedly one of the most common, most improper, and most dangerous, I thought, Sire, that I would perform a service for all good men of your kingdom if I wrote a comedy which denounced hypocrites and placed in proper view all of the contrived poses of these incredibly virtuous men, all of the concealed villainies of these counterfeit believers who would trap others with a fraudulent piety and a pretended virtue.

I have written this comedy, Sire, with all the care and caution that the delicacy of the subject demands; and so as to maintain all the more properly the admiration and respect due to truly devout men, I have delineated my character as sharply as I could; I have left no room for doubt; I have removed all that might confuse good with evil, and have used for this painting only the specific colors and essential lines that make one instantly recognize a true and brazen hypocrite.

Nevertheless, all my precautions have been to no avail. Others have taken advantage of the delicacy of your feelings on religious matters, and they have been able to deceive you on the only side of your character which lies open to deception: your respect for holy things. By underhanded means, the Tartuffes have skillfully gained Your Majesty's favor, and the models have succeeded in eliminating the copy, no matter

8

how innocent it may have been and no matter what resemblance was found between them.

Although the suppression of this work was a serious blow for me, my misfortune was nonetheless softened by the way in which Your Majesty explained his attitude on the matter; and I believed, Sire, that Your Majesty removed any cause I had for complaint, as you were kind enough to declare that you found nothing in this comedy that you would forbid me to present in public.

Yet, despite this glorious declaration of the greatest and most enlightened king in the world, despite the approval of the Papal Legate and of most of our churchmen, all of whom, at private readings of my work, agreed with the views of Your Majesty, despite all this, a book has appeared by a certain priest which boldly contradicts all of these noble judgments. Your Majesty expressed himself in vain, and the Papal Legate and churchmen gave their opinion to no avail: sight unseen, my comedy is diabolical, and so is my brain; I am a devil garbed in flesh and disguised as a man, a libertine, a disbeliever who deserves a punishment that will set an example. It is not enough that fire expiate my crime in public, for that would be letting me off too easily: the generous piety of this good man will not stop there; he will not allow me to find any mercy in the sight of God; he demands that I be damned, and that will settle the matter.

This book, Sire, was presented to Your Majesty; and I am sure that you see for yourself how unpleasant it is for me to be exposed daily to the insults of these gentlemen, what harm these abuses will do my reputation if they must be tolerated, and finally, how important it is for me to clear myself of these false charges and let the public know that my comedy is nothing more than what they want it to be. I will not ask, Sire, for what I need for the sake of my

reputation and the innocence of my work: enlightened
kings such as you do not need to be told what is
wished of them; like God, they see what we need and
know better than we what they should give us. It is
enough for me to place my interests in Your Majesty's
hands, and I respectfully await whatever you may
care to command.


## SECOND PETITION

*(presented to the King in his camp before the city
of Lille, in Flanders)*


Sire,

It is bold indeed for me to ask a favor of a great
monarch in the midst of his glorious victories; but in
my present situation, Sire, where will I find protection
anywhere but where I seek it, and to whom can I
appeal against the authority of the power that crushes
me, if not to the source of power and authority, the
just dispenser of absolute law, the sovereign judge
and master of all?

My comedy, Sire, has not enjoyed the kindnesses of
Your Majesty. All to no avail, I produced it under the
title of *The Hypocrite* and disguised the principal
character as a man of the world; in vain I gave him
a little hat, long hair, a wide collar, a sword, and lace
clothing, softened the action and carefully eliminated
all that I thought might provide even the shadow
of grounds for discontent on the part of the famous
models of the portrait I wished to present: nothing did
any good. The conspiracy of opposition revived even
at mere conjecture of what the play would be like.
They found a way of persuading those who in all other
matters plainly insist that they are not to be deceived.
No sooner did my comedy appear than it was struck

down by the very power which should impose respect; and all that I could do to save myself from the fury of this tempest was to say that Your Majesty had given me permission to present the play and I did not think it was necessary to ask this permission of others, since only Your Majesty could have refused it.

I have no doubt, Sire, that the men whom I depict in my comedy will employ every means possible to influence Your Majesty, and will use, as they have used already, those truly good men who are all the more easily deceived because they judge of others by themselves. They know how to display all of their aims in the most favorable light; yet, no matter how pious they may seem, it is surely not the interests of God which stir them; they have proven this often enough in the comedies they have allowed to be performed hundreds of times without making the least objection. Those plays attacked only piety and religion, for which they care very little; but this play attacks and makes fun of them, and that is what they cannot bear. They will never forgive me for unmasking their hypocrisy in the eyes of everyone. And I am sure that they will not neglect to tell Your Majesty that people are shocked by my comedy. But the simple truth, Sire, is that all Paris is shocked only by its ban, that the most scrupulous persons have found its presentation worthwhile, and men are astounded that individuals of such known integrity should show so great a deference to people whom everyone should abominate and who are so clearly opposed to the true piety which they profess.

I respectfully await the judgment that Your Majesty will deign to pronounce; but it is certain, Sire, that I need not think of writing comedies if the Tartuffes are triumphant, if they thereby seize the right to persecute me more than ever, and find fault with even the most innocent lines that flow from my pen.

Let your goodness, Sire, give me protection against

their envenomed rage, and allow me, at your return from so glorious a campaign, to relieve Your Majesty from the fatigue of his conquests, give him innocent pleasures after such noble accomplishments, and make the monarch laugh who makes all Europe tremble!

## THIRD PETITION

### (*presented to the King*)

Sire,

A very honest doctor, whose patient I have the honor to be, promises and will legally contract to make me live another thirty years if I can obtain a favor for him from Your Majesty. I told him of his promise that I do not deserve so much, and that I should be glad to help him if he will merely agree not to kill me. This favor, Sire, is a post of canon at your royal chapel of Vincennes, made vacant by death.

May I dare to ask for this favor from Your Majesty on the very day of the glorious resurrection of *Tartuffe*, brought back to life by your goodness? By this first favor I have been reconciled with the devout, and the second will reconcile me with the doctors. Undoubtedly this would be too much grace for me at one time, but perhaps it would not be too much for Your Majesty, and I await your answer to my petition with respectful hope.

# TARTUFFE

❧

## THE CAST

MADAME PERNELLE, ORGON'S *mother*.
ORGON, ELMIRE'S *husband*.
ELMIRE, ORGON'S *wife*.
DAMIS, ORGON'S *son*.
MARIANE, ORGON'S *daughter, in love with* VALÈRE.
VALÈRE, *In love with* MARIANE.
CLÉANTE, ELMIRE'S *brother*.
TARTUFFE, *a hypocrite*.
DORINE, MARIANE'S *maid*.
MONSIEUR LOYAL, *a bailiff*.
A POLICE OFFICER.
FLIPOTE, MADAME PERNELLE'S *maid*.
LAURENT, TARTUFFE'S *servant*.

*The scene is in Paris*

## Act I

❧

### SCENE I

[MADAME PERNELLE *and her maid,* FLIPOTE, ELMIRE,
MARIANE, DORINE, DAMIS, CLÉANTE]
[*The stage is divided into two levels of action: an
elevated level or balcony at the rear of the stage,
leading to the sleeping quarters and guest rooms; and
a large living room in the foreground on the level of*

13

*the stage, in which the principal action occurs. A stairway leads from the living room to the balcony. The living room furniture is abundant and comfortable but not ornate. Near the rear of the room and slightly to one side is a large table covered with a carpet that extends over the sides to the floor, and flanked by two arm chairs. A folding partition is at the other side of the room, near the rear corner. Doors are at opposite sides; one is alongside of a fireplace, and the other adjoins a small closet built into the wall. The wall decorations are simple, consisting chiefly of paintings, a bureau with candlesticks, and a crucifix.*

*As the curtain rises,* MADAME PERNELLE *comes down the stairs and takes her cape from the large table.* ELMIRE *follows and helps her put it on. The others remain on the balcony, and move one by one into the living room as they are addressed in turn by* MADAME PERNELLE. *She speaks in a loud and violent tone of voice while moving rapidly about the room.*]

MADAME PERNELLE. Come, Flipote, come along, so that I may be rid of them.

ELMIRE. You walk so fast that I can't keep up with you.

5   MADAME PERNELLE. Enough, Daughter-in-law, no farther please; I do not need these compliments. [*They move toward the side door.*]

ELMIRE. We do no more than our duty. But, Mother, why do you leave us so quickly?

MADAME PERNELLE. Because I can't put up with this
10 household; no one cares at all about what I say. Indeed, I am leaving here most displeased. I have been contradicted in all of my advice; nothing is respected; you all talk at the top of your voice, and it's nothing but a lot of noise.

15   DORINE. If . . .

MADAME PERNELLE. [*She turns to face* DORINE.] Sweetheart, you are a talkative, impertinent maid, and you meddle in everything just to say what you think.

DAMIS. But . . . [*He moves down the stairs toward* MADAME PERNELLE.]

MADAME PERNELLE. Son, in four letters, you're a 20 fool. I who am your grandmother tell you so; and I have a hundred times told my son, your father, that I foresaw you would be a bad sort and give him nothing but trouble. [DAMIS *moves angrily back toward the stairs but is stopped and calmed by* ELMIRE.]

MARIANE. I think . . . 25

MADAME PERNELLE. Good Heavens, Granddaughter, you pretend to be a quiet sort and look as if butter would not melt in your mouth; but as they say, still waters run deep, and you carry on in an underhanded way that I strongly detest. 30

ELMIRE. But, Mother . . .

MADAME PERNELLE. Daughter-in-law, if you please, your conduct is utterly bad. You ought to set them a good example. Their dead mother chose a much better method. You are a spendthrift and it hurts me 35 to see you go around dressed like a princess. Whoever would please none but her husband, Daughter-in-law, has no need of so much finery.

CLÉANTE. But, Madame, after all . . .

MADAME PERNELLE. As for you, her good brother, 40 I have great esteem for you, love you and revere you. But yet, if I were my son, her husband, I should firmly request that you stay away from the house. You are always preaching maxims which no honest man should follow. I am somewhat frank with you but 45 such is my nature; I never mince words.

DAMIS. Your Monsieur Tartuffe is no doubt very happy . . .

MADAME PERNELLE. [*Turning to* DAMIS] He is a good man and should be listened to. I can't stand to 50 see him railed at by a fool like you and not be angry.

DAMIS. [*His speech is rapid and excited.*] Really,

do you mean that I should let a hypocrite assume a
tyrannical power in our house? And shall we have no
55 amusement unless this pretty fellow deigns to give his
consent?

DORINE. If you listen to him and believe what he
says, you won't be able to do a thing that is not a
crime. That pious critic condemns everything.

MADAME PERNELLE. [*Addressing the whole com-*
60 *pany*] And what he condemns is very well condemned.
It is the way to Heaven that he would show you, and
my son ought to make you all love him.

DAMIS. No, good woman, I tell you that neither
father nor anything on earth can oblige me to wish
65 him well. If I said otherwise it would be a damnable
lie. His actions constantly infuriate me. I foresee consequences and am sure to come to an open quarrel
with this rogue. [*He moves toward the stairway as if
to go at once to* TARTUFFE'S *room, but is stopped and
calmed by* CLÉANTE.]

DORINE. It is truly a shame that a total stranger
70 should make himself master here, and a beggar at
that who, when he came, had not shoes on his feet,
and whose clothes all together are not worth a penny;
and such a one so far forgets himself as to twist everything around and play the master of the household.

75 MADAME PERNELLE. Ha! By Heaven above, it certainly would go better here if everything were done
according to his pious orders.

DORINE. In your mind he may be a saint, but take
my word for it, he's nothing but a hypocrite.

80 MADAME PERNELLE. [*Pointing at* DORINE] There's
a tongue for you!

DORINE. Without good security I would not trust
myself with him any more than with his man Laurent.

MADAME PERNELLE. I can't tell what the servant
85 may be but I'm sure the master is a good man. You
wish him harm and shun him only because he tells
you your faults. It is against sin that his wrath is

aroused, and the interest of Heaven is all that moves him.

DORINE. Yes, but how is it that of late he can't bear 90
that anyone should come to see us? How does an innocent visit offend Heaven that there should be such a noise about it? Shall I tell you what I think? I think he is jealous of my mistress.

MADAME PERNELLE. [To DORINE] Hold your tongue 95
and take care what you say. He is not the only one who criticizes these visits and all this hurry of visitors. Those coaches which are always at your door and the noisy gatherings of so many servants make a terrible racket in the whole neighborhood. [*She now turns and* 100
*faces* ELMIRE.] I should like to think that nothing underhanded is going on, but it is talked about, you know, and that is not as it should be.

CLÉANTE. Come now, Madame, would you keep people from talking? It would be a dreadful thing if 105
because of foolish tongues we must give up our best friends; and even were we to do so, do you think people would be any more silent? There is no defense against slander. So let us not pay attention to wagging tongues but try to live decently, and if others want 110
to talk, let them have their way.

DORINE. Our neighbor Daphne and her little husband are the ones who say such bad things about us. They whose conduct is most ridiculous are always the first to condemn others. They never fail to seize on the 115
least suspicion of an intrigue, to spread the news with great joy, and to give it just the turn that they would have people believe. They hope to cover themselves by speaking wrongly of their neighbors and, by suggesting some similarity, try to give an air of innocence 120
to their own intrigues or to make others share in that blame which is heaped upon themselves.

MADAME PERNELLE. These arguments have nothing to do with the case. Everyone knows that Orante [DORINE *and* CLÉANTE *exchange knowing smiles.*]

125 leads an exemplary life. She cares only about Heaven,
and I have been told she strongly condemns the company that comes here.

DORINE. An admirable example, truly! The lady is
good! It is true that she lives austerely; but age has
130 put this burning zeal into her soul, and she's a prude
because she's ugly. As long as she could attract men's
hearts, she enjoyed all her advantages; but seeing the
charms of her eyes decay, she now renounces the
world, which indeed renounced her, and with the
135 pompous veil of lofty wisdom she endeavors to dis-
guise the weakness of her worn-out charms. Such are
the ways of coquettes. It is painful for them to see
themselves deserted by their courtiers, and in their
desolation the only outlet for their dark discomfort
140 is the profession of virtue. The severity of these good
women censures everything and pardons nothing.
They loudly condemn everyone, not out of charity
but from an envy that cannot endure that another
should have the pleasures which their declining age
145 denies them.

MADAME PERNELLE. These are the silly stories that
you like to hear. [*Turning towards* ELMIRE] Daughter-
in-law, silence is the rule in your house, for this gentle-
woman [*She points to* DORINE.] takes over the whole
150 conversation; but I shall speak in my turn. [*Her voice
rises.*] I tell you my son never did a wiser thing than
to take home this devout man. Heaven directed him
here to reclaim you, and you should all listen to him
for your salvation. He censures nothing but what de-
155 serves to be. These visits, these balls, these meetings,
are all inventions of the evil spirit. One never hears
the least pious word. All is empty talk, trifles, and idle
tales. The neighbor is often the subject of scandal,
and the slander covers almost everybody. In short,
160 sensitive people are disturbed by the confusion of
such gatherings. As a learned man rightly said the

other day, it is really the tower of Babylon,[1] for every
one babbles there to his heart's content; [CLÉANTE
*laughs out loud.*] and to tell you a story this brings
into my head. . . . What? [*She speaks directly to*      165
CLÉANTE.] You're giggling already, are you, Sir? Go
and find your own fools to laugh at. Good-bye, Daughter-in-law, I'll say no more. [*She moves rapidly across
the room in front of the whole group.*] Know that I
have not half the esteem for this household that I        170
used to have, and it will be fine weather before I put
my foot in here again. [*Giving* FLIPOTE *a box on the
ear*] Come along there, you. You stand there dreaming and gaping in the air, but by Heaven, I shall rub
your ears for you. Come along, you sloppy thing, you,   175
come along. [*As she leaves she is followed by* ELMIRE,
MARIANE, *and* DAMIS.]


## SCENE II

### CLÉANTE, DORINE

[DORINE *from the doorway motions to* CLÉANTE *to
join the others.*]

CLÉANTE. I won't go to see her off for I fear she
will scold me again. How this good woman . . .

DORINE. [*She moves to the center of the stage.*]
Well, it is a pity she did not hear you call her so.
She'd say the same to you and add that she did not
think herself old enough yet for that title.                5

CLÉANTE. How angry she was with us for nothing!
And how fond she seems of her Tartuffe!

DORINE. Oh, all this is nothing to what the son does.
If you had seen him, you'd say it was much worse.
The troublesome times of our recent history made        10
him act like a wise man, and he showed courage in

[1] Babylon  Madame Pernelle means "the tower of Babel";
hence Cléante's laughter.

serving his Prince. [*She lowers her voice a little.*]
But he has changed into a stupid man since he became
so fond of Tartuffe. He calls him his brother, and in
15 his heart loves him a hundred times more than his
mother, son, daughter, or wife. [*She points toward*
Tartuffe's *room.*] He is the only confidant of all his
secrets and the director of his actions. He fondles
him, embraces him, and I believe no one could have
20 more affection for a mistress. At table he places him
at the upper end and is glad to see him eat as much as
six others. He must have all the best portions, and if
he happens to belch, he says to him, "God bless you."
In short, he is mad about him; he's his all, he's his
25 hero. Everything he does he admires. He quotes him
in all he says. His least actions seem miracles to him,
and every word he says is an oracle. The rogue, who
knows his dupe and wants to make the best of him,
dazzles him by a hundred different guises. His hypoc-
30 risy is constantly getting money out of him, and he
freely assumes the right of pronouncing judgment
upon every one of us. His very footboy takes it upon
himself to lecture us. He delivers sermons to us with
wild eyes and throws our ribbons, laces, and make-up
35 all over the place. The other day the wretch tore with
his very hands a neckerchief of mine because he found
it pressed in a book about saints, saying that we im-
piously mixed holiness with the devil's ornaments.

## Scene III

Elmire, Mariane, Damis, Cléante, Dorine

Elmire. [*She enters from the side, speaking.*] You
are fortunate not to have attended the lecture she
gave us at the door. I just saw my husband come in,
and, as he did not see me, I'll go up and wait for him.
[*She goes up the stairs and turns to the right of the
balcony.*]

CLÉANTE. So as not to lose time, I'll wait for him  5
here just to say hello to him.

DAMIS. [*To* CLÉANTE] Give him a hint about my sister's marriage. I suspect that Tartuffe opposes it and
urges my father to put things off. And you know the
interest I have in it. If both my sister and Valère  10
share the same feelings, his sister, you know, is dear
to me, and if . . .

DORINE. Here he comes. [*As she signals from the
side*, DAMIS *and* MARIANE *move off the stage through
the opposite door.*]

## SCENE IV

### ORGON, CLÉANTE, DORINE

ORGON. [*He hastens toward the stairs to go up to*
TARTUFFE'S *room, but stops in the center of the living
room on seeing* CLÉANTE.] Hello, my brother; how
good to see you.

CLÉANTE. I just came by, and have the pleasure of
finding you back. It is not very pleasant in the country
yet, is it?                                         5

ORGON. Dorine . . . [*To* CLÉANTE] Please, wait a
moment, Brother-in-law. Let me inquire a little into
the news of our household and relieve my mind. [*To*
DORINE] Has everything gone well during these two
days? What has happened? How is everyone?          10

DORINE. [*She moves to the center of the stage between* CLÉANTE *and* ORGON.] The day before yesterday
my mistress had a fever which lasted until night, along
with a bad headache.

ORGON. And how is Tartuffe?

DORINE. Tartuffe? Wonderful. Big and fat with  15
bright red lips and rosy cheeks.

ORGON. Poor man!

DORINE. In the evening she lost her appetite and
could not touch a bit of supper, so painful was her
headache.                                          20

ORGON. And Tartuffe?

DORINE. He supped alone in her presence and very devoutly ate up two partridges with half a leg of hashed mutton.

25  ORGON. Poor man!

DORINE. She could not get a wink of sleep all night. The fever kept her awake and we were forced to sit up with her till daybreak.

ORGON. And Tartuffe?

30  DORINE. Feeling very sleepy, he went from the dinner table to his room, and then into his warm bed, where undisturbed he slept till the next morning.

ORGON. Poor man!

DORINE. At length we prevailed upon her to be

35  bled, and that cured her at once.

ORGON. And Tartuffe?

DORINE. He took courage and, fortifying his soul against all evils, to restore the blood my mistress had lost, he drank for his breakfast four large glasses of

40  wine.

ORGON. Poor man!

DORINE. In short, both of them are very well, and I'll go up to my mistress to tell her in advance how glad you are of her recovery. [*She goes up the stairs and turns toward* ELMIRE'S *room.*]


SCENE V

ORGON, CLÉANTE

CLÉANTE. [*Moving to the center of the room*] She mocks you to your face, Brother, and I must tell you frankly without meaning to make you angry, you deserve it. Did anyone ever hear of such foolishness?

5  Has this man a magical charm to make you forget everything for him? That after you have raised him from his misery you should carry it so far as to . . .

ORGON. [*In a commanding tone*] Just a moment, Brother-in-law, you don't know the man you are talking about.

CLÉANTE. Well. I don't know him, since you will have it so; but to know what sort of a man he may be . . .

ORGON. Brother, you'd be delighted if you knew him and your joys would never have an end. [*He raises his eyes toward* TARTUFFE's *room.*] He is a man . . . who . . . hmm . . . a man . . . well, in short, a man. Whoever follows his rules enjoys a profound peace and looks upon all the world as dirt. Through his instruction I have become a changed man. He teaches me to care about nothing. He frees my soul from all affectionate feelings, and I could see my brother, children, mother, and wife die without caring a rap.

CLÉANTE. Brother, these are humane feelings!

ORGON. Oh, if you had but seen him as I first did, you would love him as I do. He came to church every day and gently kneeled on both knees just opposite me. He attracted the eyes of the whole assembly by the warmth with which he uttered his prayers to Heaven. He sighed, heaved, and every moment humbly kissed the ground; and as I was going out, he moved quickly in front of me to offer me holy water at the door. His servant, who imitated him in everything, informed me of his poverty and his former station in life, and I gave him some presents, but he would always modestly want to give me back some of them. It's too much, he would say, too much by half; I don't deserve your pity. And when I refused to take them back, he gave them to the poor before my very eyes. In short, Heaven prompted me to take him home, and since then everything seems to prosper here. He watches over everybody and even takes an extreme interest in my wife herself. He tells me of those who make eyes at her, and appears ten times more jealous of her than I am. But you won't believe

how far his piety extends. He thinks the least trifle
a sin, so much so that the other day he condemned
himself for having caught a flea as he was praying and
killed it in too great anger.

50   CLÉANTE. My word, Brother, I believe you've gone
crazy. Are you making fun of me with this sort of talk
and do you think that all this nonsense . . .

ORGON. Brother, what you say smacks of freethink-
ing. You are a little tainted with it, and as I have often
55 told you, you'll bring some sort of harm upon yourself.

CLÉANTE. This is the usual talk of such as you.
They'd have everybody as blind as themselves. To see
clearly is to be a freethinker, and he who does not
60 adore empty poses has neither respect nor faith for
sacred things! [*His voice rises as he moves toward*
ORGON.] Go, all you can say does not terrify me. I
know what I am saying and Heaven sees my heart.
I'll be no slave to all your ceremonious hypocrites.
65 There are pretenders to devotion as well as to courage;
and as those who are truly brave in battle are not
they who make the most noise, so those who are truly
devout, who ought to be imitated, are not those who
make the most outward show. Can you make no dis-
70 tinction between hypocrisy and devotion? Will you
give the same title and honor to the mask as to the
face? Will you give cunning the same value as sincerity, confound appearance with truth, esteem the
shadow as much as the substance, and false money as
75 much as good? How strangely are most men made!
They are never at one with nature. Reason's bounds
are too small for them. They exceed its limits in every
way, and often ruin the noblest of things in trying
to go too far. Let this be said by the way, Brother.
80   ORGON. Yes, you are certainly an honored sage. All
the knowledge of the world resides in you. You are
the only wise man, and oracle, a Cato of the age, and

all other men are fools by comparison. [*He turns his back to* CLÉANTE, *who again moves toward him.*]

CLÉANTE. I am no honored sage, Brother, nor has knowledge altogether come to rest in me. But in a 85 word, I can discern truth from falsehood; and as I think none are more to be prized than truly good men, as nothing in the world is nobler or finer than the holy fervor of true zeal, so nothing is more detestable than the counterfeit outside of false piety, than those 90 brazen cheats, those worshippers for show, whose sacrilege and deceitful mockery impudently abuse and make wanton sport of what mankind holds most holy and sacred. Those men who out of mean self-interest make a trade and commodity out of devotion, and 95 would purchase credit and dignity by false turns of the eyes and affected raptures, those men, I say, whom we see using the way to Heaven with unnatural warmth to make their fortune, who, while praying and burning with devotion, ceaselessly beg for alms, who 100 extol solitude in the midst of the court, who know how to reconcile their piety with their vices—these men are hasty, revengeful, faithless, cunning, and, to destroy any one who stands in their way, they insolently cover their fierce resentment with the interest of 105 Heaven; they are so much the more dangerous in their harsh wrath because they use against us arms which are revered, and their passion assassinates us with a consecrated sword. There are too many of this false character; but the truly devout are easily known. 110 Our age, Brother, shows us some who may serve as glorious examples. Look at Ariston, Periandre, Oronte, Alcidamas, Polydore, Clitandre; that title is not contested them by any. They are not braggarts in virtue. We do not behold in them any unbearable ostentation, 115 and their devotion is human and generous. They do not censure our every action. They think such admonitions savor too much of pride, and, leaving to others

the pomp of words, they correct our actions by their
120 own. They do not judge by appearances, but are
naturally inclined to think well of everyone. They do
not conspire or intrigue. To live well is their only care.
They are never provoked with the sinner but with the
sin only; they do not act with excessive zeal on behalf
125 of the interests of Heaven, but leave this care to
Heaven itself. Truly, these are good men and this is
the right practice. This is the example we ought to
propose to ourselves. But clearly, your man is not of
this model. You praise his devotion in good faith, but
130 I believe you are dazzled by a false luster.

ORGON. My dear Brother-in-law, have you finished?

CLÉANTE. Yes.

ORGON. Then I am your humble servant. [*He moves
towards the stairs.*]

CLÉANTE. [*Moving quickly in front of* ORGON] As
135 a favor, one more word with you, Brother. We'll drop
our previous discussion. You know Valère has your
promise to be your son-in-law.

ORGON. Yes. [*He turns his face away from* CLÉANTE,
*evasively.*]

CLÉANTE. You set a day for his marriage.

140 ORGON. True.

CLÉANTE. Then why do you put it off?

ORGON. I don't know.

CLÉANTE. Have you any other thought in mind?

ORGON. Perhaps. [*He begins to go up the stairs.*]

145 CLÉANTE. Would you break your word?

ORGON. I don't say that.

CLÉANTE. I trust that nothing can hinder you from
keeping your promise.

ORGON. That may be.

150 CLÉANTE. Is there need of all this mystery to say one
word? Valère has sent me to you about it.

ORGON. Heaven be praised for that.

CLÉANTE. But what answer shall I give him?

ORGON. What you will.

CLÉANTE. But it is necessary to know your plans. 155
What are they?

ORGON. To do what Heaven wills.

CLÉANTE. But let us speak seriously. Valère has your
word. Will you keep it or not?

ORGON. [*From the balcony*] Good-by. 160

CLÉANTE. [*Alone*] I fear misfortune to his love, and
I must warn him about all that is happening. [He *goes
out through the side door as the curtain falls.*]

# Act II

❧

## Scene I

### Orgon, Mariane

Orgon. [*Coming from the balcony*] Mariane.

Mariane. Yes, Father?

Orgon. Come over here. I have something to say to you in private.

5　Mariane. What are you looking for?

Orgon. [*Looking into a little closet*] I am seeing whether anyone is here to listen, for this little place might easily conceal someone. So, we're safe. Mariane, I have alwaye found you good natured, and you have

10　always been dear to me.

Mariane. I'm very much obliged to you for your fatherly love.

Orgon. That's very good, my Daughter, and to deserve it you ought to do nothing but what will please

15　me.

Mariane. There is nothing that I want more.

Orgon. Very well. What do you say of Tartuffe, our guest?

Mariane. Who, I?

20　Orgon. Yes, you. Take care how you answer.

Mariane. Alas! I'll say whatever you like. [Dorine *enters quietly and stands behind* Orgon *without being seen.*]

Orgon. You speak wisely. Say then, Daughter, that a high merit shines in all his person, that he touches your heart, and that you should be glad to see him

25　become, by my choice, your husband. Well?

MARIANE. [*Jumping back in surprise*] What?
ORGON. What is it?
MARIANE. What did you say?
ORGON. What?
MARIANE. Was I mistaken?                                    30
ORGON. How?
MARIANE. Who is it, Father, you would have me
say touches my heart? Whom should I be glad to see
become, by your choice, my husband?
ORGON. Tartuffe. [DORINE *motions to* MARIANE *to* 35
*challenge her father's view.*]
MARIANE. I'll swear, Father, he has no share in my
heart. Why would you have me tell a lie?
ORGON. But I'll have it a truth. It is enough for you
that I have ordered it.
MARIANE. [*In tears*] Oh, Father! Do you want . . . 40
ORGON. Yes, Daughter. I plan to unite Tartuffe to
our family by your marriage. He shall be your husband. I have resolved upon it, and as I have absolute
power over . . . [ORGON *notices* MARIANE'S *distrac-*
*tion, turns, and sees* DORINE]                             45

## SCENE II

### DORINE, ORGON, MARIANE

ORGON. [*Stepping back*] What are you doing there?
Your curiosity must be strong indeed, my girl to make
you listen to us like this.
DORINE. Truly, I don't know whether the rumor
comes from conjecture or guess, but I was told about 5
this marriage and laughed at it as sheer nonsense.
ORGON. What, then, is it so incredible?
DORINE. So much so that I would not believe you,
yourself, Sir, if you should tell it to me.
ORGON. I know the way to make you believe it.      1C
DORINE. Oh, yes, you are telling a funny story.

ORGON. I am telling you precisely what you shall very soon see.

DORINE. A joke.

15     ORGON. What I say, Daughter, is not in jest.

DORINE. Don't believe your father. He is joking.

ORGON. I tell you . . .

DORINE. No, don't bother; no one will believe you.

ORGON. I am getting so angry now that . . . [*He moves menacingly toward* DORINE.]

20     DORINE. [*Stepping back*] Very well. We believe you, and so much the worse for you. Is it really possible, Sir, that you who seem to be such an intelligent person can be fool enough to want to . . . ?

ORGON. Look here, my girl, you have taken certain
25 liberties which I don't like at all.

DORINE. Please Sir, let us speak without anger. Are you poking fun at people in this affair? Your daughter is not made for this bigot. He has other things to think of, and besides, what good can such an alliance do
30 you? Why should a man of your fortune choose a beggar . . .

ORGON. Hold your peace. The poorer he is, the more he ought to be respected. His misery is certainly an honest misery and lifts him above all worldly grandeur,
35 since he lost his estate only by his too little care for temporal things and his powerful attachment to eternity. But my help may give him the way to get out of his trouble and regain his possessions. They are properties that are valued highly in his province, and poor
40 as he is, he's a gentleman.

DORINE. Yes, so he says, and that vanity, Sir, does not agree with the piety he professes. He who embraces the innocence of a holy life ought not to boast so much of his name and birth, and the humble ways
45 of devotion will not well endure that sort of ambition. What good does this pride do? [*Orgon moves sharply toward* DORINE.] . . . But this talk offends you. Let's speak of his person and leave out his nobility. Could

you have the heart to make such a man as he possessor
of a girl like her? Ought you not to consider decency 50
and forsee the consequences of this union? A woman's
virtue is in danger when she is married against her
will, for her desire to live properly depends upon the
qualities of her mate, and cheated husbands who are
laughed at often make their wives what they are. 55
[ORGON *signals* MARIANE *not to listen and to turn
away from* DORINE.] In short, it is very hard to be
faithful to certain kinds of husbands, and he that gives
his daughter to a man she hates is answerable to
Heaven for the faults she commits. Think of what 60
dangers your plan forces on you.

ORGON. I tell you she must learn from me how to
live.

DORINE. You can do no better than to follow my
instructions. 65

ORGON. [*To* MARIANE] Let us not amuse ourselves,
Daughter, with these trifles. I know what's best for
you and I am your father. It is true that I had consented to Valère for you, but besides that I hear he's
given to gambling, I suspect him to be somewhat of 70
a freethinker, for I do not see him often at church.

DORINE. Would you have him run there at your pre-
cise hours, like those who go for nothing but to be
seen?

ORGON. [*He turns toward* DORINE.] I don't ask for 75
your advice about it. [*To* MARIANE] In short, the other
is on the best of terms with Heaven, and that makes
him as rich as anyone. This marriage will bring you
the greatest of glories and your life will be filled with
nothing but sweetness and pleasure. [ORGON *takes* 80
MARIANE's *hands.*] You'll live together happily like
two babes in arms, like two turtle doves. You'll never
quarrel, and you may make what you will of him.

DORINE. She? She'll make nothing but a cuckold of
him, I assure you. 85

ORGON. What talk is this?

DORINE. I tell you he has the look of one already, and his destiny, sir, will carry the day over all your daughter's virtue.

90 ORGON. Stop interrupting me and hold your tongue, without putting your nose into other people's business.

DORINE. I speak, Sir, only for your interest.

[*She continually interrupts him every time he turns to speak to his daughter.*]

ORGON. You go to too much trouble; be quiet, if you please.

95 DORINE. If I did not like you . . .

ORGON. I do not care to be liked.

DORINE. [*Moving toward* ORGON] But I like you, Sir, in spite of yourself.

ORGON. Ah!

100 DORINE. Your honor is dear to me, and I can't bear that you should let yourself be laughed at by everyone.

ORGON. Won't you hold your tongue!

DORINE. It would be a sin to let you contract such an alliance.

105 ORGON. [*Angrily*] Will you shut up, serpent, whose impudent . . .

DORINE. Ah, but you are a religious man and you are losing your temper.

ORGON. [*Speaking more calmly*] Yes, this nonsense 110 provokes me, and I will absolutely have you hold your peace.

DORINE. Be it so. But if I don't speak, I'll still go on thinking.

ORGON. Think if you will, but take care you don't 115 speak or else [*He hesitates for a moment.*] . . . enough said. [*Turning to his daughter*] I have considered everything carefully.

DORINE. I am furious that I cannot speak. [*She's silent when he turns his head.*]

ORGON. Though Tartuffe is not handsome, yet his 120 person is such . . .

DORINE. Yes, he's a fine piece indeed.

ORGON. That though you had not the slightest regard for all his other gifts . . . [*He turns to* DORINE *and looks at her with his arms folded.*]

DORINE. A fine prize she'll get truly, but if I were in her place a man would not marry me by force and 125 get away with it, and soon after the wedding I'd let him know that a woman always has her revenge ready.

ORGON. So. You pay no attention to what I say?

DORINE. What are you complaining about? I'm not talking to you. 130

ORGON. What are you doing then?

DORINE. I'm talking to myself.

ORGON. Very well. I must give her a blow to punish her rash insolence. [*He puts himself in position to slap her but at every glance of his eye,* DORINE *remains silent.*] Daughter, you should approve of my de- 135 sign . . . Think of the husband . . . that I have chosen for you . . . [*To* DORINE] Why don't you speak?

DORINE. I have nothing to say to myself.

ORGON. Just one little word. 140

DORINE. It doesn't suit me.

ORGON. To be sure, for I'm watching you. [*He turns back to* MARIANE.]

DORINE. Some fool, by jove.

ORGON. Well, my Daughter, you ought to show obedience and entire deference to my choice. 145

DORINE. [*Moving away*] I'd be hanged before I'd have such a husband.

ORGON. [*Tries to give her a blow and misses*] You have a plaguey wench there, Daughter, and without sinning I can't bear with her any longer. I am now in 150 no condition to go on. Her insolent remarks have inflamed me, and I'm going outside to calm myself a little.

## Scene III

### Dorine, Mariane

Dorine. [*Coming back to the center of the room*] Really, have you lost your tongue? Do I have to play your part? To hear such an insane proposal without making even the slightest answer!

Mariane. What would you have me do against the
5 absolute power of a father?

Dorine. What you must to counter such a threat.

Mariane. But what?

Dorine. You should have told him that nobody loves by proxy; that you will marry for yourself and not for
10 him; that as you are the person principally concerned, the husband ought to please you rather than your father; that if he thinks Tartuffe so charming he may marry him himself.

Mariane. A father has so much power over us that
15 I have never had the strength to say a word against him.

Dorine. But let's come to the point. [*She speaks in a more intimate tone.*] Valère has taken steps to obtain you. Tell me, do you love him or not?

20 Mariane. How great, Dorine, is your injustice to my love! Ought you to ask me that? Have I not opened my heart to you a hundred times, and don't you know how I feel about him?

Dorine. How could I know that your heart spoke
25 through your lips and that this lover really affected you?

Mariane. You wrong me, Dorine, in doubting it. My true feelings have been only too apparent.

Dorine. You love him then?

30 Mariane. Desperately.

Dorine. And he seems to love you no less?

Mariane. I think so.

DORINE. And both of you want to be married?

MARIANE. Certainly.

DORINE. Then what is your intention concerning the 35 other marriage?

MARIANE. [*She hesitates for a moment.*] To kill myself if I am forced to it.

DORINE. Very good. That is a way out I had not considered. You need only die, and your troubles are 40 over. The remedy is certainly wonderful! I really get angry when I hear people talk this way. [*She walks rapidly around the room with* MARIANE *after her.*]

MARIANE. Good Heavens! What a fit you are in, Dorine. You are not very kind to those in trouble.

DORINE. [*She stops and turns to* MARIANE.] I can't 45 treat stupidity with kindness and weaken at a moment of crisis as you do.

MARIANE. But what do you expect? If I am timid . . .

DORINE. But love requires firmness.

MARIANE. Do I lack constancy to Valère? And is it 50 not his business to obtain me from my father?

DORINE. [*Moving toward* MARIANE] But what if your father is a downright ass, completely captivated by his Tartuffe, and breaks his promise? Is it your lover's fault? 55

MARIANE. But shall I by a flat refusal and an outburst of scorn seem to be too much in love? And no matter how attractive Valère may be, should I go beyond the modesty of my sex and abandon a daughter's duty? And would you have my love made public . . . ? 60

DORINE. No, no. I'd have nothing. I see you have a mind to be Tartuffe's and I would be wrong, now that I think about it, to keep you from such an alliance. Why should I oppose your inclinations? The match in itself is most advantageous. Monsieur Tartuffe! Well 65 now, is he a nobody? Indeed, Monsieur Tartuffe, if we take it aright, is no ordinary fellow, and it is no small happiness to be his wife. Everyone already crowns him with glory. He is a nobleman in his own

70 part of the world, well-made in his person, his ears
pink and his complexion rosy; you'll live only too
happily with such a husband.

MARIANE. [*Moving toward* DORINE] My God! . . .

DORINE. What inner joy you will have when you
75 see yourself the wife of so fine a man.

MARIANE. Please stop, I beg you, and show me a
way out of this marriage. I give up, and am ready to
do whatever you want me to.

[*She takes* DORINE's *hands, but* DORINE *releases herself and moves away.*]

DORINE. No. A daughter must obey her father. Do
80 you think he'd marry her to a monkey? Your lot is a
happy one. What are you complaining about? You'll
go in a stagecoach to his home town, which you'll
find flourishing with uncles and cousins. And you
will enjoy talking to them. They'll take you into high
85 society. You shall visit the bailiff's wife and the tax-
collector's wife who will honor you with the hardest
chair in their living rooms. At carnival time, you may
expect a ball with full orchestra: to wit, two bagpipes,
and sometimes an ape and marionettes. If, however,
90 your husband . . .

MARIANE. [*In tears*] You are killing me. You ought
to think of helping me.

DORINE. I'm your servant.

MARIANE. Please, Dorine . . .

95 DORINE. No. I must let this affair go on, to punish
you.

MARIANE. Dear girl!

DORINE. No.

MARIANE. If my wishes . . .

100 DORINE. No. Tartuffe's your man and have him you
shall.

MARIANE. You know I have always confided in you.
Tell me . . .

DORINE. No. By the Lord, you shall be Tartuffed.

105 MARIANE. Well, since my fate cannot move you,

leave me alone to my despair, and from it my heart
will draw help. I know an infallible remedy for all my
misfortunes. [*Starts to go out*]

DORINE. [*Holding her arms out to Mariane*] Well,
well, come back, I am not angry any more. In spite of  110
everything, I must take pity on you.

MARIANE. Don't you see, Dorine, if I am put to that
cruel torment, I tell you I will die.

DORINE. Do not torment yourself. We can skilfully
prevent . . . but here comes Valère, your lover.          115

## SCENE IV

### VALÈRE, MARIANE, DORINE

VALÈRE. [*Going directly to* MARIANE] I was just
told a strange piece of news, my lady, which I did not
know before, and which is certainly very fine.

MARIANE. What is it?

VALÈRE. That you're to marry Tartuffe.                     5

MARIANE. [*After a brief pause*] Indeed, my father
has such a plan in mind.

VALÈRE. Your father . . .

MARIANE. Has changed his mind. He just now proposed it to me.                                            10

VALÈRE. What! Seriously?

MARIANE. Yes, seriously. He declared himself openly
for this marriage.

VALÈRE. And what are your wishes?

MARIANE. I do not know. [*At this reply* DORINE    15
*shrugs her shoulders, turns, and goes up to the bal-
cony.*]

VALÈRE. An honest answer. You do not know?

MARIANE. No.

VALÈRE. No?

MARIANE. What advice would you give me?

VALÈRE. I should advise you to accept this husband.  20

MARIANE. You advise me to do it?

VALÈRE. Yes.

MARIANE. Seriously?

VALÈRE. Of course. The choice is splendid and de-
25 serves to be taken seriously.

MARIANE. Very well, Sir, this is a piece of advice that
I'll accept.

VALÈRE. I doubt that you'll have much trouble following it.

30 MARIANE. No more than you had in giving it.

VALÈRE. I gave it to please you, my lady.

MARIANE. And to please you I take it. [*She turns her
back to him.*]

DORINE. [*Aside*] Let's see what will come of this.
[*She moves to the front of the balcony and leans for-
ward.*]

VALÈRE. So this is how you love? And it was a lie
35 when you . . .

MARIANE. [*Turning to* VALÈRE] Please, let's talk no
more of that. You told me frankly that I ought to accept the man who was proposed to me for a husband,
and I say that I intend to do it, since you have given
40 me such wholesome advice.

VALÈRE. Don't excuse yourself with what I said.
You had already made up your mind and you seize
on the slightest pretext to support your breaking your
word.

45 MARIANE. Truly, that is well said.

VALÈRE. Certainly. And your heart never had any
real warmth for me.

MARIANE. Well! You are perfectly free to think so.

VALÈRE. Yes, yes, I am perfectly free. But my of-
50 fended feelings may find a similar way out and I
know where to bestow my vows and my hand.

MARIANE. I don't doubt it, and the passions aroused
by merit . . .

VALÈRE. My Lord! No talk of merit. I have certainly
55 very little and you will agree, but I have confidence in
the kindness another will have for me [MARIANE,

*startled, moves slightly toward him.*] and I know one whose heart will be open to me and who will freely consent to repair my loss.

MARIANE. The loss is not great, and, as for the 60 change, you will console yourself easily enough.

VALÈRE. If I can I will, you may be sure of it. To be rejected in love affects our pride. We must make every effort to forget it. If we cannot, we must at least pretend to, and it is unpardonably mean to show love 65 for one that has cast you off.

MARIANE. The sentiment is certainly noble and sublime.

VALÈRE. Good enough. Everyone will approve it. Come, now, would you have my passion burning for 70 you forever, and would you have me see you given to the arms of another without bestowing elsewhere a heart you have refused?

MARIANE. On the contrary, I'd have you do it. I wish it were done already. 75

VALÈRE. You wish it?

MARIANE. Yes. [*She turns her back to him.*]

VALÈRE. I have been insulted enough, my lady, and will satisfy you on the spot. [*He moves toward the door and then returns.*]

MARIANE. Very well. 80

VALÈRE. Remember, however, that you force me to this extremity.

MARIANE. Yes.

VALÈRE. And that my design is forced only by your example. 85

MARIANE. By my example; be it so.

VALÈRE. Enough, you shall be punctually obeyed.

MARIANE. So much the better.

VALÈRE. You see me for the last time in my life.

MARIANE. [*Without looking at* VALÈRE] Fine. 90

VALÈRE. [*Goes, and when he reaches the door, turns toward* MARIANE.] What was that?

MARIANE. [*Turning toward* VALÈRE] What?

VALÈRE. Didn't you call me?

MARIANE. I? You are dreaming. [*She turns away again.*]

95 VALÈRE. Well then, I'll be on my way. Farewell.

MARIANE. Farewell, Sir.

DORINE. [*She comes rapidly down the stairs and moves toward* VALÈRE.] For my part your silly talk makes me think you have lost your senses. I let you quarrel only to see how far it would go. Here now, 100 good VALÈRE! [*She tries to hold him at the door by the arm, and* VALÈRE *seems to resist strongly.*]

VALÈRE. What? What do you want, Dorine?

DORINE. Come here.

VALÈRE. No. No. My feelings are too strong. [*He moves toward the door.*] Don't hinder me from doing 105 what she would have me do.

DORINE. Stay.

VALÈRE. No, I am resolved.

DORINE. Ah! [*She drags* VALÈRE *toward the center of the room, and* MARIANE *moves to the opposite side.*]

MARIANE. It pains him to see me. My presence drives 110 him away, and I rather than he should be the one to leave.

DORINE. [*Leaves* VALÈRE *and runs to* MARIANE] The other one! Where are you running?

MARIANE. Let me go. [*She opens the door to go out.*]

115 DORINE. You must come back.

MARIANE. No, no, Dorine. It's useless to try to hold me.

VALÈRE. I see that the very sight of me disturbs her. I had better relieve her pain. [*He moves again to the the opposite door.*]

DORINE. [*Leaves* MARIANE *and runs to* VALÈRE] 120 Again? The devil with you if I let you do it. Stop this nonsense and come here, both of you. [*She pulls first one and then the other, bringing them both toward the center of the stage.*]

VALÈRE. But what's the idea?

MARIANE. What do you mean to do?

DORINE. To reconcile you and straighten things out. [*To* VALÈRE] Are you mad to have had such a quarrel? 125

VALÈRE. Didn't you hear how she talked to me?

DORINE. [*To* MARIANE] Are you stupid to be carried away like that?

MARIANE. Didn't you see how he treated me?

DORINE. Stupidity on both sides. [*To* VALÈRE] I am 130 sure that she has no other desire than to keep herself for you. [*To* MARIANE] He loves you alone, and wishes only to be your husband. I'll stake my life upon it.

MARIANE. Then why should he give me such advice?

VALÈRE. Why should you ask me for such advice? 135 [*They turn their backs on one another.*]

DORINE. You are both crazy. Come give me your hands, both of you. [*To* VALÈRE] Yours.

VALÈRE. [*Giving* DORINE *his hand*] What do you want with my hand?

DORINE. [*To* MARIANE] Come now, yours. 140

MARIANE. [*Giving her hand*] What is this all about?

DORINE. [MARIANE *and* VALÈRE *still have their backs to one another.*] Come, come quickly. You love one another more than you imagine. [*She places* VALÈRE'S *hand in* MARIANE'S; *they turn face to face and smile.*]

VALÈRE. [*To* MARIANE] But don't be so difficult, and look upon me openly. [MARIANE *looks lovingly at* 145 VALÈRE.]

DORINE. Really, lovers are quite mad.

VALÈRE. [*Suddenly releasing* MARIANE'S *hand*] Have I not reason to complain of you? Truthfully, were you not wrong to upset me so?

MARIANE. But are you not the most ungrateful 150 man . . . ?

DORINE. [*Coming between them*] Let's put off this debate to another time, and think how to ward off this annoying marriage.

MARIANE. Tell us then what means we must use. 155

DORINE. We must use all manner of means. Your

father is greatly deceived, but you had better seem
to consent placidly to his stupidity, so that if need be,
you may the more easily drag out this proposal. We
160 can fix everything by gaining time. First you must
claim you have a sudden illness which requires delay.
Then you must pretend ill omens: you were upset by
a meeting with a dead man, or you broke a looking
glass, or dreamt of muddy water. The best of it all is
165 that you can never be married without saying yes. But
the better to succeed, it is best that you two should not
be seen talking together. [*To* VALÈRE] Go and without
delay stir up your friends to make him keep his promise to you. [*She pushes him toward the door.*] We'll
170 go and arouse his brother and get the stepmother on
our side. Farewell.

VALÈRE. [*To* MARIANE] Whatever means we may
employ, my greatest hope is in you.

MARIANE. [*To* VALÈRE] I cannot answer for my
175 father's will, but I'll never belong to anyone but
Valère.

VALÈRE. How glad you make me! and whatever
may dare . . .

DORINE. Lovers are never tired of talking. [*She
180 pushes* VALÈRE *again.*] Go, I say.

VALÈRE. [*He takes a step, then turns and rejoins*
MARIANE.] In short . . .

DORINE. What a babbler your lover is! [*Pushing
each of them by the shoulder*] You go out this way;
you, the other. [*They go out at opposite doors as the
curtain rapidly falls.*]

# Act III

## Scene I

### Damis, Dorine

Damis. [*Entering quickly*] May thunder strike me dead! May I be used everywhere like the worst of rogues if any law or power hold me back and if I do not blow up altogether.

Dorine. Please, control yourself a little. Your 5 father has only talked of it yet. Saying is one thing and doing is another, and it's a long way from the plan to the event.

Damis. I must check that wretch's plot and speak a word or two in his ear. [*He moves toward the rear* 10 *stairway as if to go up to* Tartuffe's *room.*]

Dorine. [*Blocking* Damis' *way*] Be calm. Let your stepmother handle him and your father. She has some effect on Tartuffe. He is agreeable to all she says, and perhaps may feel some passion for her. Would to Heaven it were so! It would be a fine situation! In 15 short, your concern has made her send for him. She intends to sound him out about the marriage that disturbs you, discover his feelings, and show him what terrible confusion he may bring about if he lends any support to this plan. His servant says he's at prayers 20 but that he'll come down soon. Please go out and let me wait for him. [*She pushes him toward the door.*]

Damis. [*Resisting*] I must be present at their conversation.

Dorine. By no means. They must be left alone. 25

Damis. I won't say a word to him.

DORINE. You are mistaken. We know your hot temper. It would be the best way to ruin everything. Leave.

30 DAMIS. I won't. I will see what goes on and I won't get angry.

DORINE. How troublesome you are. Here he comes. Go. [*She pushes him to the door. As soon as* DORINE'S *back is turned,* DAMIS *loudly slams the door and then slides along the wall to the closet, which he enters noiselessly.*]

## SCENE II

### TARTUFFE, LAURENT, DORINE

TARTUFFE. [*As he comes down the stairs he sees* DORINE, *who turns her back to him.*] Laurent, put away my hair shirt and my scourge, and pray that Heaven may always enlighten you. If anybody comes to see me, I have gone to the prisoners to distribute 5 alms.

DORINE. [*Turning toward* TARTUFFE] What affectation and deceit!

TARTUFFE. What do you want?

DORINE. To tell you . . .

TARTUFFE. [*Takes a handkerchief out of his pocket* 10 *which he holds out to* DORINE] Oh my God, please, take this handkerchief before you speak.

DORINE. For what?

TARTUFFE. [*His eyes raised upward*] Cover that bosom which I cannot bear to see. The sight of such 15 objects wounds the soul and gives rise to guilty thoughts.

DORINE. Surely, you are easily tempted, and the flesh makes a great impression upon your senses. I cannot tell how hot you may be, but I do not take fire 20 so quickly, and I could see you naked from head to toe without being tempted by any part of you.

TARTUFFE. Be a little modest in your talk, or I'll leave you at once. [*He turns toward the door.*]

DORINE. No, no, I'll leave you. I have but one word to say to you. My mistress is coming down into this 25 parlor and desires to talk with you.

TARTUFFE. Oh, with all my heart.

DORINE. [*To herself*] How soft he becomes! I do believe I have always guessed right.

TARTUFFE. [*Turning toward* DORINE] Will she come 30 soon?

DORINE. I think I hear her. Yes, it's she. I'll leave you together. [ELMIRE *comes down from the balcony as* DORINE *goes out.*]

## SCENE III

### ELMIRE, TARTUFFE

TARTUFFE. [*Rushing to meet* ELMIRE] May Heaven in its infinite goodness always give you health in both soul and body, and bless your days as much as is wished by the most humble of those whom its love inspires.

ELMIRE. I am very much obliged to you for this 5 pious wish, but let's take a chair so that we may talk more easily. [*She sits down, and* TARTUFFE *pulls his chair alongside of hers.*]

TARTUFFE. How do you feel now after your illness?

ELMIRE. Very well. The fever soon left me. 10

TARTUFFE. My prayers are not worth so much as to draw down this favor from above, but I have not uttered a single word that had not your recovery for its object.

ELMIRE. Your piety disturbed itself too much for 15 me.

TARTUFFE. Your dear health is priceless. I would give my own to have redeemed it.

ELMIRE. You carry Christian charity very far, and I owe you a great deal for all this goodness. 20

TARTUFFE. I do much less for you than you deserve.

ELMIRE. I want to speak to you secretly about a certain matter, and I am glad nobody is near to hear us.

25 TARTUFFE. I am thrilled in finding myself alone with you. It is a favor I have often begged of Heaven, but till now it has never been granted me.

ELMIRE. All that I ask of you is a word or two of open and honest conversation. [DAMIS *opens the closet door slightly without being seen.*]

30 TARTUFFE. And I too, for this special favor, wish but to reveal to you all of my heart and my soul, and I swear that my objection to the attention paid to your charm is by no means the result of any hatred for you, but is rather the effect of a pious emotion which 35 carries me away, and of a pure movement . . .

ELMIRE. So I take it, and believe that my salvation gives you this concern.

TARTUFFE. [*Squeezing the tips of her fingers*] Yes, certainly, Madame, and so great is my fervor . . .

40 ELMIRE. [*Pulling back her hand*] Ouch! You squeeze me too hard.

TARTUFFE. From excess of zeal. I had never intended to do you any harm, and I'd sooner . . . [*He puts his hand upon her knee.*]

ELMIRE. What is your hand doing there?

45 TARTUFFE. I'm feeling your clothes. The material is very soft.

ELMIRE. Please stop; I'm very ticklish. [*She draws back her chair, and* TARTUFFE *pulls his after her.*]

TARTUFFE. How wonderful is this lace work. They work miraculously nowadays. Never was anything so 50 well made.

ELMIRE. That is so. But let's talk of our business a little. It is said that my husband wants to go back on his word and give you his daughter. Tell me, is it true?

55 TARTUFFE. He said a little to me about it, but to

tell the truth, Madame, that is not the happiness I
sigh for; and I see elsewhere the wonderful charms
which alone can make me happy.

ELMIRE. That is because you love no earthly things.

TARTUFFE. [*Smiling at* ELMIRE] My breast does not 60
enclose a heart of stone.

ELMIRE. For my part, I believe that your sighs are
all for Heaven, and that nothing here below can en-
gage your desires.

TARTUFFE. The love that binds us to eternal beau- 65
ties does not keep us from the love of temporal ones.
Our senses may easily be charmed by the perfect
works which Heaven has formed. Its reflected charms
shine in yours, but it displays in your person its
rarest wonders. Upon your face it has diffused beauty 70
which surprises the eye and transports the heart. And
I could not behold you, perfect being, without ad-
miring in you the author of nature and feeling my
heart touched with a burning love for the most
beautiful of portraits which Heaven paints of itself. 75
At first I feared that this secret passion was a clever
temptation of the evil spirit, and therefore resolved
even to avoid your sight, thinking you an obstacle
to my salvation; but now I know, oh lovely beauty,
that this passion cannot be guilty, that it may be 80
reconciled with virtue, and this makes me abandon
my heart to it. I confess, it is bold indeed for me to
dare to offer my heart to you, but it is your goodness
alone that gives me hope, and not the empty long-
ings of my weakness. In you is all my hope, my happi- 85
ness, my peace; on you depends my torment or my
joy, and by your sole decree I shall be either happy
or miserable.

ELMIRE. [*After a moment's hesitation*] The declaration is extremely gallant, but to tell you the truth, it 90
is a little surprising. I think you should have fortified
your spirit and reflected a little upon such a design.
A devout man like you, whom everyone calls . . .

TARTUFFE. I'm nonetheless a man because I'm de-
95 vout, and when one beholds your heavenly charms, he
lets himself be caught without reflecting on the matter. I know that such a discourse must seem strange
coming from me, but Madame, after all, I'm no
angel, and if you condemn this confession you ought
100 to blame your entrancing charms. As soon as I was
dazzled by their more than human splendor, you became the ruler of my being. The ineffable sweetness
of your divine glances triumphed over the resistance
of my heart. It overcame my fasting, prayers, and
105 tears, and turned all my desires toward your charms.
My eyes and my sighs have told it to you a thousand
times, and for a better explanation I now use my
voice. If therefore you contemplate with a little kindness the tribulations of your unworthy slave, if your
110 goodness will deign to comfort me and descend to my
lowliness, I shall forever, oh, delicate miracle, be de-
voted to you beyond all comparison. Your honor runs
no risk with me and has no disgrace to fear on my
part. All those court gallants whom women so madly
115 adore are loud in what they do and vain in what they
say. They are continually boasting of their conquests.
They divulge every favor they receive, and their
indiscreet tongue, which has been entrusted with confidence, dishonors the altar on which they sacrifice
120 their hearts. But men of our sort burn with a discreet
flame, and a secret is always safe with us. The care
we take of our reputation is a secure pledge to the
one we love. And it is in us they find, when they accept our hearts, love without scandal and pleasure
125 without fear.

ELMIRE. I hear all that you say, and your eloquence
is clear enough. But are you not afraid that I might
care to acquaint my husband with this gallant passion
and that the speedy notice of such a love may readily
130 alter the friendship he has for you?

TARTUFFE. I know you have too much goodness,

and that you will pardon my rashness; that you will
ascribe to human weakness the violent feelings of
a love that offends you, and consider that I am not
blind and that a man is of flesh and blood. [*He pulls* 135
*his chair closer to* ELMIRE, *who rises and moves*
*slightly away.*]

ELMIRE. Perhaps another would act differently, but
I'll show my discretion. I'll say nothing to my husband,
but in return you must do something for me: that is
to aid openly and without hesitation the marriage of
Valère with Mariane, to renounce the unjust power 140
which would enrich you with the possession of what
belongs to another, and . . .

## SCENE IV

### ELMIRE, DAMIS, TARTUFFE

DAMIS. [*Coming out of the little closet in which he*
*was hiding*] No, Madame, no, this must be made
known. [*Triumphantly*] I was concealed in this place
where I could hear everything, and Heaven's goodness
seemed to have led me there to confound the pride
of a traitor who seeks my ruin, to open a way for me 5
to take revenge for his hypocrisy and insolence, to
undeceive my father and show him in broad daylight
the character of a wretch who talks to you of love.
[TARTUFFE *rises as* DAMIS *closes the closet door be-*
*hind him.*]

ELMIRE. [*Placing herself between* DAMIS *and* TAR-
TUFFE] No, Damis, it is enough that he grow wiser
and try to deserve the pardon I agree to. Since I have 10
promised him, don't make me break my word. It is
not my nature to make a scene. A woman laughs at
such foolishness and never bothers a husband over it.

DAMIS. You have your reasons for doing so, and
I have mine too for doing otherwise. It is a joke to 15
think of sparing him, and the insolence of his bigotry

has triumphed too long over my just wrath and caused
only too much confusion here. The cheat has governed
my father too long already, and has harmed my love
20 and Valère's. He must know the truth about this
wretch and Heaven offers me an easy way to let him
know it. I am obliged to it for this opportunity, and
it is too good a one to neglect. I should deserve to
lose it if, now that I have it in my hand, I did not
25 make use of it.

ELMIRE. Damis . . .

DAMIS. No, if you please, I must follow my own
inclinations. My spirits are crowned with joy, and
your attempt to make me give up the pleasure of
30 revenge is useless. Without further ado I will settle
this business, and here precisely is my opportunity.
[ORGON *enters from the side door.* TARTUFFE *takes a
breviary from his pocket and begins to pray.*]

## SCENE V

### ORGON, DAMIS, TARTUFFE, ELMIRE

DAMIS. [*Rapidly*] Father, we are going to celebrate
your arrival with a story that is piping hot, and that
will greatly surprise you. You are well paid for all
your caresses, and this gentleman rewards your kind-
5 ness most richly. His great zeal for you just now declared itself. He will do nothing less than dishonor
your bed, and I surprised him making a confession
of his guilty love to your wife. She is rather gentle
and too discreet, and would have kept it secret, but
10 I could not tolerate such impudence, and believe that
to keep it from you is to wrong you. [ORGON *looks at*
DAMIS *and then at* TARTUFFE, *whose eyes are on his
prayer book.*]

ELMIRE. Indeed, I think we should never disturb a
husband's rest with such idle nonsense. Honor does
not depend upon that, and it is enough for us to know

how to protect ourselves. These are my views and, 15
if I could have prevailed upon you, Damis, you would
have said nothing about it. [*She goes up to the balcony and leaves the scene.*]

## SCENE VI

### ORGON, DAMIS, TARTUFFE

ORGON. [*In a low voice, to* TARTUFFE.] O Heavens!
Is this credible?

TARTUFFE. [*He hesitates a moment while he finishes
his prayers; then he closes his book, puts it into his
pocket, and turns toward* ORGON.] Yes, Brother, I am
a wretch, a criminal, an unhappy sinner filled with
iniquity; the greatest villain that ever was. Every mo- 5
ment of my life is soiled with pollution. [*He advances
toward* ORGON *with outstretched arms.*] It is all a
heap of crimes and filthiness, and I see that Heaven,
for my punishment, means to mortify me on this occasion. [*He crosses his arms on his chest.*] However 10
great the forfeit may be, I am not so bold as to defend myself. Believe what is told you. [*He points to*
DAMIS.] Arm your wrath and drive me out of your
house like a criminal. [*In tears, and beating his chest*]
I cannot be put to as much shame as I deserve. 15

ORGON. Ah! [*Turning to his son*] Traitor, do you
dare by this lie to try to stain the purity of his virtue?

DAMIS. What! [*Moving toward* ORGON] Can the
pretended meekness of this hypocrite make you disbelieve . . . 20

ORGON. [*Menacingly*] Hold your tongue, cursed
wretch.

TARTUFFE. Oh, let him speak. You blame him wrongfully; you would do better to believe what he tells
you. Why should your view be so favorable to me? 25
After all, do you know what I may be capable of
doing? Do you trust merely in my appearance,

Brother? Do you think me any the better for what you
see of me? No, no, you allow yourself to be deceived
30 by appearances, and alas, I am far from what you
think I am. Everyone takes me for a good man, but
the truth is, I'm a good-for-nothing. [*Turning to*
DAMIS] Yes, my dear son, speak on. Call me wretched,
infamous, lewd, a thief, a murderer. Overwhelm me
35 with names yet more detestable. I will not contradict
you; I have deserved them, and upon my knees I will
suffer humiliation as a shame that the crimes of my
life have earned. [*He ends in tears and falls to his
knees.*]

ORGON. [*To* TARTUFFE] Brother, this is too much.
40 [*To his son*] Will not your heart relent, traitor?

DAMIS. What! Do his words so far deceive you . . .

ORGON. Hold your tongue, rogue. [*To* TARTUFFE]
Pray, Brother, rise. [*To his son*] Wretch!

DAMIS. Can . . .

45 ORGON. Quiet!

DAMIS. I can't bear it! I am taken for . . .

ORGON. If you say another word, I'll break your
bones.

TARTUFFE. Brother, in the name of God, do not be
50 angry. I'd rather suffer the most severe of pains than
have him receive the least scratch on my account.

ORGON. [*To his son*] Ungrateful wretcn!

TARTUFFE. Let him alone. If I must ask his pardon
upon my knees, I'll . . . [*He falls to his knees again.*]
55 ORGON. [*To* TARTUFFE] You jest? [ORGON *also falls
to his knees and the two embrace.*] See his goodness,
scoundrel.

DAMIS. Then . . .

ORGON. [*Rising*] Quiet!

60 DAMIS. What! I . . .

ORGON. Quiet, I say! I know what makes you insult
him. You all hate him. Today I see my children and
my servants all set against him. [TARTUFFE, *still on his
knees, takes hold of* ORGON's *coat and weeps.*] They

impudently practice every trick to remove this good 65
man from me, but the more they try to get him away,
the harder I will try to keep him; and therefore I'll go
and hasten his marriage with my daughter so that I
may confound the pride of my whole family. [TAR-
TUFFE *rises*]

DAMIS. Are you going to make her accept him? 70

ORGON. Yes, villain, on this very evening too, to
spite you. I defy you all and give you notice that I am
to be obeyed, that I am the master. Come, eat your
words, good-for-nothing, and throw yourself at his
feet to ask his pardon, at once. 75

DAMIS. Who? I? [DAMIS *begins to move away, and*
ORGON *seizes hold of him.*] Ask pardon of that impostor, who by his deceit . . .

ORGON. What! Do you resist, beggar, and abuse him!
A stick! A stick! [*To* TARTUFFE] Don't hold me. [*To* 80
DAMIS] Out of my house at once, and don't ever dare
to set foot in it again.

DAMIS. Yes, I'll go, but . . . [*He looks steadily at*
TARTUFFE, *who smiles.*]

ORGON. [*Pushing* DAMIS *toward the door*] Quick,
out of here. I disinherit you, wretch, and give you 85
my curse. [DAMIS *goes out.*]

## SCENE VII

### ORGON, TARTUFFE

ORGON. [*Closing the door and returning to the center of the room*] To offend a holy person in this manner!

TARTUFFE. O Heaven, forgive him for the pain he
inflicts upon me. [*To* ORGON] If you knew how it
makes me feel to see them try to blacken me in the 5
eyes of my Brother . . .

ORGON. Alas! [*He takes hold of* TARTUFFE's *hands.*]

TARTUFFE. The mere thought of this ingratitude is

such punishment for my soul. . . . The horror of it
10 all. . . . [*He places his hand on his heart.*] My heart
is so swollen that I cannot speak, and I believe that
I will die of it. [TARTUFFE *collapses into an arm chair.*]

ORGON. [*Runs in tears to the door out of which he
drove his son.*] Villain! I regret that my hand spared
you and did not break your bones upon the spot.
15 [*Returning to* TARTUFFE] Come, be yourself, Brother,
and do not grieve.

TARTUFFE. Let us put an end to these annoying dis-
turbances. I see what trouble I cause here, and I think,
Brother, that I had best be gone.

20 ORGON. What? You do not mean it?

TARTUFFE. I am hated here and I see they try to
make you doubt my sincerity.

ORGON. What does it matter? You see how I mind
them.

25 TARTUFFE. They certainly will not stop trying, and
these same stories which you now reject, you may
perhaps take more seriously another time.

ORGON. No, Brother, never.

TARTUFFE. Oh, Brother, a wife may easily mislead
30 a husband.

ORGON. No, no.

TARTUFFE. Let me, by leaving at once, deprive
them of any cause for attacking me thus. [*He moves
toward the door.*]

ORGON. No, you shall stay, I pledge my life upon
35 it.

TARTUFFE. [*He stops and turns to* ORGON.] Well,
then, I must mortify myself. Yet, if you will . . .

ORGON. Ah!

TARTUFFE. Be it so. Let's mention it no more. But
40 I know what I must do about it. Honor is a delicate
thing, and friendship requires me to prevent rumors
and avoid causing trouble. I will shun your wife's
presence, and you shan't see me . . .

ORGON. No, in spite of them all, you shall be with

her often. My greatest joy is to infuriate them, and 45
I'll have you be seen with her all the time. And this
is not all. The better to defy them, I will have no
other heir but you, and I'll go immediately and sign
over to you a deed to all my property. A good and
loyal friend, whom I take for my son-in-law, is much 50
dearer to me than my son, wife, or relatives. Will you
not accept my offer?

TARTUFFE. Heaven's will be done in all things.

ORGON. Alas! Poor man! Come, let's get a deed
drawn quickly, and let them burst with envy. [*They* 55
*leave at the side door as the curtain quickly falls.*]

# Act IV

## SCENE I

### CLÉANTE, TARTUFFE

[*As the curtain rises,* CLÉANTE *has just come into the living room, where he finds* TARTUFFE.]

CLÉANTE. Yes, everyone is talking about it, and you may believe me, this story does you no credit. And I'm glad, Sir, that I happened to meet you, so that I can tell you quite briefly what I think about it. I won't
5 consider what has been alleged. I pass that by and take matters at their worst. Suppose Damis did not act properly and accused you wrongfully, is it not the part of a Christian to pardon offenses and to suppress all thoughts of revenge? And should you let a son be
10 thrown out of his father's house because of your quarrel? I must tell you again without mincing words, everyone, whether rich or poor, is ashamed of it, and if you take my advice, you will restore peace to the household and not drive matters to a head. Sacrifice
15 your resentment to Heaven and return the son to his father's favor.

TARTUFFE. Alas! For my part, I'd do it with all my heart. I bear him no ill will, Sir. I forgive him everything, blame him for nothing, and would serve him
20 to the utmost of my power. But the interest of Heaven would not consent to it, and if he comes here again I must be gone. After his unheard-of behavior, any relations between the two of us would lead to trouble. God knows what people might believe. They would
25 think it pure policy on my part, and everyone would

say that, knowing myself in the wrong, I pretend a charitable sympathy for my accuser, that I fear him and want to bargain with him by bribing him into silence.

CLÉANTE. [*Moving toward* TARTUFFE] These ex- 30 cuses are good for nothing. All your arguments, Sir, are too farfetched. Why do you take Heaven's interests upon yourself? Does Heaven need us to punish the guilty? Leave to it the care of its revenge. Think only of the pardon it enjoins to offenses, and pay no 35 attention to what men say when you follow the sovereign orders of Heaven. Come now, shall this pointless concern over what people might think hinder us from doing good? No, no, let us always do what Heaven prescribes and not trouble our heads with 40 anything else.

TARTUFFE. I have already told you that my heart pardons him, and that, Sir, is what Heaven commands. But after this scandal and affront, Heaven does not order me to live with him. 45

CLÉANTE. And does it order you, Sir, to agree with what pure caprice prompts a father to do? And to accept the gift he makes you of an estate to which you have no right?

TARTUFFE. Those who know me will not hold it a 50 selfish deed. All the riches of the world have no charms for me. I am not dazzled by their false luster, and, if I do resolve to receive the father's gift, it is only, to tell you the truth, because I am afraid his estate may fall into the wrong hands; that those who 55 share in it may use it for criminal ends and not employ it as I intend, for the glory of Heaven and the good of my neighbor.

CLÉANTE. My good Sir, do not have these delicate fears which may cause a lawful heir to complain. Let 60 him, without troubling yourself, run the risk of possessing his estate, and consider that it were better that he misused it than that you should be accused of de-

priving him of it. But I am amazed that you should
65 entertain such an idea without feeling disturbed, for
has true piety any rule which sanctions disinheriting
a lawful heir? And if Heaven has made you feel that
it is impossible to live with Damis, shouldn't you dis-
creetly make an honorable retreat from this house
70 rather than thus permit an only son to be unreason-
ably turned out-of-doors on your account? Believe me,
sir, this reflects strangely on your integrity, and . . .
[Tartuffe *looks at his watch.*]

TARTUFFE. It is half past three, Sir. Certain pious
duties call me upstairs, and you will excuse me if I
75 leave you so soon.

CLÉANTE. Ah! [*As* TARTUFFE *leaves by the rear
stairway,* DORINE *comes in from the side door, followed by* MARIANE *in tears, supported by* ELMIRE.

## SCENE II

### ELMIRE, MARIANE, DORINE, CLÉANTE

DORINE. [*To* CLÉANTE] Please, Sir, help us for
Mariane's sake. Her heart has suffered a mortal
blow. [CLÉANTE *embraces and trys to comfort*
MARIANE.] The match her father has concluded for
5 tonight drives her almost to despair. He is coming
soon. I beg of you, let us join our forces and try, by
force or cunning, to alter the unhappy plan that has
upset us all.

## SCENE III

### ORGON, ELMIRE, MARIANE, CLÉANTE, DORINE

[ORGON *enters from the opposite side, holding the
contract of marriage.*]

ORGON. Oh, I'm glad to find you all together. [*To*
MARIANE] I have something here in this contract that
will make you smile. You already know what it means.

MARIANE. [*On her knees*] Father, in the name of Heaven who knows my grief and by all that can move your heart, give up a little of your paternal power, and free my love from this obedience. [ORGON *turns his face away.*] Do not compel me by this hard law to complain to Heaven for what I owe you. Do not, my Father, make the life you have given me unhappy. [MARIANE *is almost overcome with tears.*] If in spite of the sweet hopes I once had, you forbid me to be his whom I have dared to love, I implore you on my knees, at least save me from the torment of being his whom I abhor, and do not drive me to some desperate act by using all of your power over me.

ORGON. [*Feeling himself moved*] Be firm, my heart. Show no human weakness.

MARIANE. It is not your affection for your favorite that disturbs me. Give it full sway. Give him your estate, and, if that is not enough, add all mine to it. I consent with all my heart, and leave it all to you; but I pray you, do not include me as well, and let me spend in a convent the sad days that Heaven has decreed me. [*She bursts into tears again.*]

ORGON. [*Turning to* MARIANE] Ah! You're one of that sort of nuns who cloister themselves as soon as their father crosses them in love. Get up. [*He seizes her hand and pulls her up.*] The more it goes against your grain to accept him, the more merit you will have in taking him. Mortify your senses with this marriage, and do not trouble my head about it any more.

DORINE. [*Moving toward* ORGON] But . . .

ORGON. Quiet, you. Mind your own business. I forbid you to speak a single word. [DORINE *turns and goes up the stairs, but remains on the balcony, watching.*]

CLÉANTE. If you'll allow me to answer with a little advice . . .

40 ORGON. Brother, your advice is the best in the world
and I value it highly, but I must beg your pardon if
I don't take it. [CLÉANTE *moves over to* MARIANE'S
*side.*]

ELMIRE. [*To her husband*] I don't know what to
say to all this. I am amazed at your blindness. You
45 must be fond of him indeed and wholly prejudiced in
his favor to refuse to believe what happened just now.

ORGON. I am your servant and believe in what
seems true. I know your affection for my rascal of a
son, and you were afraid to disown the trick he would
50 have played that poor man. You seemed too calm
to be believed. You should have been disturbed in
quite a different way.

ELMIRE. Must our honor rush to take up arms over
a simple declaration of passion? And cannot we an-
55 swer all that touches it, without fire in our eyes and
invective in our mouth? For my part I merely laugh
at such things, and do not care to make a noise over
them. I prefer that we display our wisdom gently, and
do not hold at all with those savage prudes whose
60 honor is armed with claws and teeth, who at the
slightest word are for scratching out people's eyes.
Heaven preserve me from such wisdom! I prefer virtue that is not diabolical, and think that the discreet
coldness of a blunt refusal is powerful enough to repel
65 an amorous attack.

ORGON. Well, I know the whole story and the trick
won't do.

ELMIRE. [*She advances toward* ORGON. *As she passes
the large table, she raises and then releases the carpet
covering it, and smiles.*] Again I marvel at this curious
weakness. But what would your incredulity be like
70 if I should make you see that we have told you the
truth?

ORGON. See?

ELMIRE. Yes.

ORGON. All nonsense.

ELMIRE. [*Tapping gently on the carpeted table*] But 75
what if I should show it to you plainly?

ORGON. Fairy tales.

ELMIRE. What a man you are! At least, answer me.
I don't expect you to believe me, but suppose we
could make you see it all clearly and on the spot, what 80
would you then say of your pious man?

ORGON. Then, I'd say—I'd say nothing, for it can't
be.

ELMIRE. Your error has lasted too long, and it is just
too much to be accused of deceit. For sheer pleasure 85
and without further ado, I must make you witness all
that has been told you.

ORGON. Be it so. I take you at your word. We shall
see your cunning and how you can fulfill this promise.

ELMIRE. [*Motioning to* DORINE] Bring him to me. 90

DORINE. His mind is alert and perhaps it will be
hard to catch him.

ELMIRE. No, no, a man is easily taken in by his
desires, and conceit often aids in the deception. Send
him down to me. [*To* CLÉANTE *and* MARIANE] Please 95
go out. [*She walks with them to the side door and
shuts it behind them.*]

## SCENE IV

### ELMIRE, ORGON

ELMIRE. Come here and get under this table.

ORGON. [*With marked amazement*] What did you
say?

ELMIRE. You absolutely have to hide.

ORGON. [*Approaching* ELMIRE] But why under this 5
table?

ELMIRE. Good Heavens! Just do it. I have my reason
for it, and you will see later. [*Raising the carpet of
the table*] Get under there, I tell you, and take care
that you are not seen nor heard. 10

ORGON. I must admit that my condescension is very great in this, but I have to follow you to the end of this business. [*He gets down on his hands and knees and crawls under the table. He then turns around and holds the carpet up, so that his head is visible.*]

ELMIRE. I am quite sure you won't have anything
15 to say to me about it afterwards. I am going to behave strangely, but don't be at all offended. Whatever I may say I must be allowed to say it, for it is to convince you as I have promised. I will proceed gently, since I must, to make this hypocrite lay aside his
20 mask, flatter the bold desires of his love, and provide an open field for his rashness. As it is only to satisfy you and to confound him more surely that I will pretend to respond to his desires, I will stop as soon as you yield, and matters will go no farther than you care
25 to let them. It is for you to check his insane passion when you think the affair carried far enough, to spare your wife and to expose me to no more than is necessary to undeceive you. This is all in your interest and you will be in charge. And . . . Here he comes.
30 Be still and take care not to be seen. [ORGON *rapidly pulls in his head and lets the carpet fall.*]

## SCENE V

TARTUFFE, ELMIRE, ORGON, *hidden under the table*

TARTUFFE. [*Coming from the stairs*] I was told that you want to talk to me here.

ELMIRE. I do. I have a secret to reveal to you. But shut the door first and look around to make sure that
5 we won't be surprised. [TARTUFFE *goes to close the side door and then returns. While* ELMIRE *speaks, he looks in the closet and all around the room.*] Such a scene as just took place must not be repeated here. I never saw anything like it. Damis made me very much afraid for you, and you saw that I did all I

could to destroy his plan and to calm his rage. In- 10
deed, I was so disturbed that I never thought of
contradicting him; but thank Heaven it all turned out
the better for that, and everything is more secure. The
esteem in which you are held made the storm disappear; my husband can have no suspicion of you. The 15
better to defy public scandal, he wants us to be together all the time, and by that means I may, without
fear of blame, be shut up alone with you here and
am able to open to you my heart, which is perhaps
a little too eager to receive your passion. 20

TARTUFFE. [*Looking strangely at* ELMIRE] This
language is very hard to understand, Madame; you
spoke somewhat differently a little while ago.

ELMIRE. If that refusal made you angry, how little
you know a woman's heart, or what it means when 25
she makes so weak a defense. At such moments our
modesty always combats the rise of tender emotions.
However a woman may explain an overpowering love,
she cannot admit it without a tinge of shame. [*Moving
toward* TARTUFFE] At first we defend ourselves, but 30
by the way we do so, we show that our heart yields,
that our mouth opposes our desires from a sense of
honor, and that such refusals promise everything. This
is doubtless a very free confession to you and a serious
departure from the strict rules of modesty, but, since 35
I have made it, can you see why I did not try to
keep Damis from speaking? I ask you, would I have
listened so softly to your long declaration of love,
would I have taken it as I did, had I not been pleased
with it? And when I myself tried to force you to re- 40
fuse the marriage that had just been proposed, what
should you have understood by it but my interest in
you and my regret that this tie would divide a heart
I desired to have wholly to myself? [ELMIRE *comes
up to* TARTUFFE, *but just as he is about to seize her,
she moves away.*]

TARTUFFE. It is indeed, Madame, an extreme pleasure 45

to hear these words from a mouth one loves. Their
honey diffuses through all my senses a sweetness that
I never before tasted. [ELMIRE *leans against the
table and taps on it gently.*] The joy of pleasing you
50 is my most glorious occupation, and my heart founds
its bliss upon your love. But that heart desires the
freedom of daring to doubt its happiness just a little.
I may take your words as an honorable artifice to
oblige me to break off the impending marriage, and,
55 if I may freely express myself to you, I can have no
confidence in such gentle phrases unless a few of your
favors, after which I sigh, assure me of the truth of
all you have said and plant in my heart a permanent
proof of the enchanting kindness you have for me.
[*He seizes* ELMIRE *by the waist.*]

ELMIRE. [*She releases herself and coughs to warn
60 her husband.*] Come now. Are you in such a hurry and
would you exhaust all the tenderness of a heart at
once? I have done all I could to make you the softest
confession, yet this is not enough for you; are you
not satisfied unless matters are driven to the last
65 extremity? [*She coughs again and taps on the table.*]

TARTUFFE. [*As he speaks he moves toward* ELMIRE,
*who moves backward around the table.*] The less one
deserves a happiness, the less one dares hope for it.
Our desires can hardly be satisfied by words alone.
One may readily doubt an existence that is completely
70 filled with glory; it must be enjoyed before it can be
believed. As for me who hold myself so undeserving
of your goodness, I am not sure of a happiness due to
my boldness, and I'll believe nothing, Madame, until
you have responded concretely to my passion. [*He
seizes* ELMIRE *by the waist.*]

75 ELMIRE. [*Freeing herself and retreating*] My God!
How like a tyrant your love behaves! And how it con-
fuses me! What furious power it seizes over one's
heart, and how violently it asks what it desires!
[TARTUFFE *tries to grab her hands but fails.*] Can't I

defend myself from your pursuit? Will you not give 80
me time to breathe? Does it become you to be so
relentless? To give no quarter? And thus, by your in-
sistent pressure, to take advantage of the weakness
you know that one has for you? [TARTUFFE *takes hold
of* ELMIRE's *hands and tries to pull her toward the
partition at the rear of the room.*]

TARTUFFE. But if you look on my addresses favor- 85
ably, why do you refuse me positive proof of your
disposition?

ELMIRE. [*Freeing herself*] But how can I consent
to what you want without offending Heaven, of which
you speak so often? 90

TARTUFFE. [*Again attempting to pull her toward the
partition*] If nothing but Heaven is in the way of my
desires, I can easily remove such an obstacle. That
should not restrain your heart.

ELMIRE. [*Freeing herself again*] But we are threatened so with Heaven's judgment! 95

TARTUFFE. [*Pursuing* ELMIRE *around the table*] I
can make those ridiculous terrors disappear, Madame,
and I know the way to remove all scruples. [ELMIRE
*coughs.*] It is true that Heaven forbids certain gratifi-
cations;[2] but there are ways of arranging matters. In 100
some cases there is a way to loosen the strict ties of
our conscience, and to rectify the harm of the action
by the purity of our intention. I can instruct you in
these secrets, Madame. Be ruled by me, indulge my
desires, and have no fear. I'll answer for everything 105
and will take the sin upon myself. You cough a great
deal, Madame.

ELMIRE. Yes, it is very bad.

TARTUFFE. [*Reaching into his pocket*] Would you
like a piece of this licorice? 110

ELMIRE. It is a persistent cold, I fear, and all the
licorice in the world will do no good.

---

[2] At this point of the text Molière adds the comment: [*It is a
rogue who speaks*].

TARTUFFE. It is certainly very disturbing.

ELMIRE. More than I can express.

115     TARTUFFE. In short, your scruple may easily be destroyed. I can assure you of absolute secrecy; evil is only what is made public. The scandal is what makes the crime, and sinning in private is no sin.

ELMIRE. [*After coughing again*] I see I must resolve
120 to yield; that I must grant you everything and that nothing less will content you. It is indeed hard to go so far and I do it against my will, but, since you are determined to have it so and refuse to believe all that I have said, and since more convincing evidence
125 is required, I must agree to satisfy you. [*Turning toward the table*] If this consent carries any guilt with it, so much the worse for him that forced me to it. The fault should certainly not be laid at my door.

TARTUFFE. [*He takes* ELMIRE's *hand and begins to lead her to the partition.*] I assure you, Madame, I
130 take it completely upon myself, and the deed itself . . .

ELMIRE. [*Drawing back her hand*] Please, open the door a little and see if my husband is not in that hall.

TARTUFFE. [*Seizing her hand again*] What need
135 have you to worry about him? Between ourselves, he's a man we may lead by the nose. [ELMIRE *coughs.*] He will take pleasure in all our conversations, and I have brought him to the point where he might see everything and yet believe nothing.

140     ELMIRE. No matter. [*She pushes* TARTUFFE *toward the side door.*] Do go out for a moment, please, and look carefully all around. [TARTUFFE *goes out.*]


SCENE VI

ORGON, ELMIRE


ORGON. [*He raises the carpet and crawls out from under the table.*] I must confess, this is an abominable

man. I can't get over it. The whole business over-
whelms me.

ELMIRE. Well! Are you out so soon? You won't give
anyone a chance. Go under the table again. It's not 5
time yet. Stay to the end to be absolutely sure, and put
no trust in mere conjectures.

ORGON. [*Rising to his feet*] No, nothing more
wicked ever came out of hell.

ELMIRE. My God, you should not believe so easily. 10
Be convinced before you yield, and be not so hasty
for fear of being wrong. [*The side door opens. She
puts her husband behind her, and turns toward* TAR-
TUFFE.]

## SCENE VII

### TARTUFFE, ELMIRE, ORGON

TARTUFFE. [*Advancing with outstretched arms*]
Everything conspires to my satisfaction, Madame. I
have looked over the whole apartment. Nobody is
there, and my ravished soul . . . [*As he reaches out
for* ELMIRE, *she quickly moves aside.*]

ORGON. [*Stopping him*] Gently now. [ORGON *seizes*
TARTUFFE *and holds him, although he tries to escape.*]
You pursue your amorous desires too fast, and you 5
should not be so hot. Ah, ha, my Saint, you'd make
a fool out of me, would you? How you abandon yourself to temptations! [*He flings* TARTUFFE *away from
him.*] Marry my daughter and lust after my wife!
I have long doubted that all was well, and I always 10
thought there would be some change; but this is
carrying the proof of it far enough. I am convinced
and I need no more evidence.

ELMIRE. [*To* TARTUFFE] It is against my nature
that I've done all this, but I was forced to deal with 15
you in this way.

TARTUFFE. What! Do you believe . . .

ORGON. [*Opening the side door*] Come now, if you please, no more noise; get out at once and without 20 ceremony.

TARTUFFE. My aim . . .

ORGON. This talk is out of fashion. You must leave the house right now.

TARTUFFE. [*Slowly and deliberately*] It is you who 25 must leave, you who speak like the man in charge. [*Advancing on* ORGON] I'll have you know that this house belongs to me, and I'll show you that using these low tricks to pick a quarrel with me won't do; you won't gain a thing by attacking me, for I have 30 the means to confound and punish the duplicity, revenge the offense to Heaven, and make those who bid me be gone regret it. [*He leaves rapidly.*]

## SCENE VIII

### ELMIRE, ORGON*

ELMIRE. What kind of talk is this and what does he mean?

ORGON. My word, I am confused; it isn't very funny.

ELMIRE. [*Coming closer to* ORGON] What?

5 ORGON. I see my fault by what he says, and the deed troubles me no end.

ELMIRE. The deed?

ORGON. Yes. It's done. But something else disturbs me too.

10 ELMIRE. What's that?

ORGON. You will know everything. But let's go up-stairs at once and see if a certain little box is still there. [*He mounts the steps rapidly and goes off the side of the balcony.* ELMIRE *follows as the curtain falls.*]

# Act V

❧

## Scene I

### Orgon, Cléante

[Orgon *rushes down the stairs into the living room, followed by* Cléante.]

Cléante. Where are you going so fast?

Orgon. Alas, I hardly know.

Cléante. I think we had better begin by discussing what we can do about the situation.

Orgon. That little box is my greatest worry. It 5 bothers me much more than all the rest.

Cléante. That little box, then, is an important mystery?

Orgon. My poor friend, Argas, gave it to me himself as a great secret. He chose to leave it with me when 10 he fled, and he told me it held papers which concerned his life and all he owned.

Cléante. Then why did you let someone else get hold of them?

Orgon. It was a matter of conscience with me. I 15 confided in my traitor, and he persuaded me to give him the box to keep, so that in case of some inquiry I might have a ready subterfuge whereby my conscience may safely swear contrary to the truth.

Cléante. If one may believe appearances, you're 20 in a bad way, and this deed and trust were ill-advised steps on your part. You can be used badly by means of such pledges, and with this man having such a great advantage over you, it was another piece of imprudence for you to turn him out. You should 25 have taken more peaceful steps.

ORGON. How could he conceal a heart so false, a soul so wicked under the cloak of piety! When I found him, he was a penniless beggar . . . I tell you,
30 I am through with pious men. Henceforth I will fear them like the plague and will be worse than a devil to them.

CLÉANTE. Yes, these are your violent passions. You never can keep calm about anything. Your way is
35 never that of right reason, but always runs from one extreme to the other. You see your error and have recognized that you were deceived by a counterfeit piety, but why, as a punishment on yourself, should you fall into a greater error and confound all good
40 men with a vicious wretch? Because a scoundrel dupes you brazenly under the false pretense of austere piety, do you think that all are like him and that there are no truly devout men nowadays? Leave these foolish inferences to unbelievers, distinguish virtue from
45 its mere appearances, never risk your admiration too quickly, and always keep to the middle way. Take care, if you can, not to honor imposture, but do not wrong true piety, and if you must go to extremes, sin rather on the side of indulgence.

## SCENE II

### DAMIS, ORGON, CLÉANTE

[DAMIS *first enters slowly, then rushes to his father.*]

DAMIS. Tell me, father, is it true that you are threatened by a scoundrel? That he forgets all your favors and that his base pride, which deserves your just anger, turns your own kindness into a weapon
5 against you?

ORGON. Yes, Son, and I suffer terribly from it.

DAMIS. Leave it to me and I'll cut off his ears. We must not flinch before his insolence. It is for me to free you from him at one blow, and, in order to put

an end to the business, I'll knock his brains out. 10
[DAMIS *turns to go out, but is checked by* CLÉANTE.]

CLÉANTE. You talk just like a young man. If you please, moderate these outbursts of passion. We live under a reign and in an age in which violence does only harm to one's cause.

## SCENE III

MADAME PERNELLE, MARIANE, ELMIRE, DORINE, DAMIS, ORGON, CLÉANTE

[*The ladies enter the room from the stairway.*]

MADAME PERNELLE. What is this all about? I hear the strangest tales.

ORGON. They are recent events which my eyes have witnessed. You see how I am rewarded for my good- ness. I piously embrace a man assailed by poverty, 5 I lodge him and esteem him as my very brother, load him daily with kindnesses, give him my daughter and all I have; and all the while the vicious wretch tries to seduce my wife, and not content with these low attempts, dares to threaten me with what he owes 10 to my kindness, and will take advantage of my care- less generosity in order to ruin me, to drive me from my estate which I transferred to him, and reduce me to that very condition from which I rescued him.

DORINE. Poor man! 15

MADAME PERNELLE. My Son, I cannot believe that he would commit so black a crime.

ORGON. What?

MADAME PERNELLE. Good people are always envied.

ORGON. What are you trying to say, Mother? 20

MADAME PERNELLE. There are queer things happen- ing in your house, and you know only too well how much they hate him. [*She points to the others.*]

ORGON. What has this hate to do with what you have heard? 25

MADAME PERNELLE. I told you a hundred times when you were little, that virtue is always persecuted in this world; the envious may die but envy never.

ORGON. But how does all this concern us now?

30 MADAME PERNELLE. They may have made up a hundred foolish stories against him.

ORGON. I have already told you that I saw it all myself.

MADAME PERNELLE. The malice of scandalous 35 people is boundless.

ORGON. [*Advancing on* MADAME PERNELLE] You'll make me mad, Mother. I tell you I saw this outrageous crime with my own eyes.

MADAME PERNELLE. [*Moving backward slightly*] Their tongues always have poison to spread from 40 which nothing in this world below is free.

ORGON. This conversation makes no sense at all. [*He moves toward her again.*] I have seen it, I tell you, seen it! With my own eyes, seen it! What you call "seen." Must I tell it to you a hundred times!

45 MADAME PERNELLE. Appearances often deceive. You must not always judge by what you see.

ORGON. [*Turning away*] I am going mad.

MADAME PERNELLE. Nature is subject to groundless suspicions. And good is often interpreted as evil.

50 ORGON. [*Turning again toward his mother*] Should I interpret his desire to embrace my wife as a charitable act?

MADAME PERNELLE. You should have just cause before you accuse anyone, and you should have stayed 55 till you had made sure of the outcome.

ORGON. What the devil, how could I be more certain? You'd have had me stay, Mother, till before my very eyes he had . . . You'll make me say something very stupid.

60 MADAME PERNELLE. In short, his soul is possessed by too pure a zeal, and I cannot possibly imagine how he could attempt what you say he did.

ORGON. I am so angry that if you were not my mother, I don't know what I would say to you.

DORINE. Turn-about, sir, is fair play. You would 65 believe nobody, and now others will not believe you.

CLÉANTE. [*Moving toward the center*] We lose time in trifles when we should use it to take steps. We must not sleep when we are confronted with the threats of a scoundrel.                              70

DAMIS. Would he have the nerve to go so far?

ELMIRE. It seems to me that any rights he had to the property are canceled by his open ingratitude.

CLÉANTE. Don't count on it. He'll be clever enough to make what he does seem right, and men have been 75 embroiled and confused in conspiracies for much less than this. I tell you once more, armed with what he had, you should not have pushed him so far.

ORGON. True enough, but how could I help it? I could not control my resentment at the traitor's pride. 80

CLÉANTE. I should be very glad if some sort of compromise could be arranged between you two.

ELMIRE. If I had known that he had such weapons I would not have given cause for such trouble, and my . . . [*The side door opens. All turn toward it as* 85 MONSIEUR LOYAL *appears. He is carrying a briefcase.*]

ORGON. [*To* DORINE] What does that man over there want? Go and find out. I'm in fine condition to have visitors! [DORINE *motions to* LOYAL, *who enters slowly.*]

## SCENE IV

### MONSIEUR LOYAL *and the rest*

MONSIEUR LOYAL. [*In a low and obsequious tone of voice*] Good day, my dear Sister; I beg of you, allow me to speak to your master.

DORINE. He has company and I'm afraid that he can't see anyone right now.

MONSIEUR LOYAL. I don't come to be troublesome. 5

I believe my coming will not displease him. And I come for a purpose which will relieve him very much.

DORINE. Your name?

MONSIEUR LOYAL. Only tell him that I come from
10 Monsieur Tartuffe, for his good.

DORINE. [*To* ORGON] It is a man with most polite manners, who comes from Monsieur Tartuffe, for a purpose which he says will relieve you very much.

CLÉANTE. You must see who this man is and what
15 he wants.

ORGON. Perhaps he comes to make a compromise. How should I act toward him?

CLÉANTE. You must not let your anger break out, and if he talks of an agreement, listen to him.

20    MONSIEUR LOYAL. [*To* ORGON] Good health, Sir. Heaven destroy those who mean you harm, and be as favorable to you as I could wish.

ORGON. [*To* CLÉANTE] This mild beginning confirms my judgment and suggests a compromise.

25    MONSIEUR LOYAL. Your family was always dear to me, and I was a servant to your father.

ORGON. Sir, I am ashamed and beg your pardon, that I know neither you nor your name.

MONSIEUR LOYAL. I am called Loyal, a native of
30 Normandy, and a bailiff, and I care very little that others envy me. For forty years, thank Heaven, I have had the good fortune to exercise my office with considerable honor, and I come to you, Sir, by your leave, to signify the execution of a certain decree. [*He takes out a sheet of paper from his briefcase.*]

35    ORGON. What! Do you come to . . . [ORGON *attempts to seize the paper but* LOYAL *moves it away.*]

MONSIEUR LOYAL. Sir, no excitement. This is only a summons, an order to clear out of here, you and yours, to remove your goods and make room for others without delay or postponement, as need requires.

40    ORGON. I? Leave this place?

MONSIEUR LOYAL. Yes, Sir, if you please. The house

at present, as you well know, belongs undisputedly
to the good Monsieur Tartuffe. [*Looking at the paper
as he speaks*] Henceforth he is master and lord of
your estate, by virtue of a deed which I possess. It is 45
in proper form and cannot be contested.

DAMIS. [*Approaching* LOYAL] Truly, this impudence is great, and I marvel at it.

MONSIEUR LOYAL. [*Turning to* DAMIS *and then
back to* ORGON] Sir, I have nothing to do with you,
but with this gentleman who is reasonable and tem- 50
perate. He knows the duty of a good subject too well
to oppose justice in any way.

ORGON. But . . .

MONSIEUR LOYAL. Yes, I know that you would not
rebel for a million, and that, like a true gentleman, 55
you'll let me execute my orders.

DAMIS. You may well bring down a stick upon your
black coat, Monsieur bailiff.

MONSIEUR LOYAL. Sir, let your son either be quiet
or be gone. I should be sorry to be obliged to take 60
out my notebook and see you put into my written
report. [CLÉANTE *leads* DAMIS *aside and calms him.*]

DORINE. [*Aside*] This Monsieur Loyal looks very
disloyal.

MONSIEUR LOYAL. I have great affection for all good 65
men, Sir, and would not have taken the papers except
to oblige you and do you good, to prevent someone
else from being chosen for the occasion who, not
having the regard I have for you, might have proceeded less mildly. 70

ORGON. And what can be worse than ordering
people to be gone from their homes?

MONSIEUR LOYAL. You are allowed time. And until
tomorrow, Sir, I shall suspend the execution of the
warrant. I'll only come and spend the night here with 75
ten of my men, without any disturbance or noise. As
a mere formality you must let me have the keys to
your door before you go to bed. I will take care not

to disturb your sleep and will see that nothing im-
80 proper occurs. But tomorrow, early in the morning
you must be ready to empty the house to the last
piece of furniture. My men will help you, and I have
strong ones so that they may be of more service to
you. It seems to me that you could not be dealt with
85 better, and, as I treat you with great indulgence, I
strongly request you to behave properly and not to
disturb me in the execution of my duty.

ORGON. [*Turning to* ELMIRE *and in a low voice*]
Right now I would give with all my heart a hundred
of the best gold pieces I have left for the pleasure of
90 smashing in that snout. [*He begins to move toward*
LOYAL *but* ELMIRE *holds him back.*]

CLÉANTE. [*In a low voice, to* ORGON] Be careful;
let's not make things worse.

DAMIS. [*Moving about, agitatedly*] In the face of
this insolence I can hardly hold myself back, and my
95 hand itches.

DORINE. By my faith, Monsieur Loyal, a few strokes
of a club would not sit badly upon your good back.

MONSIEUR LOYAL. Such vulgar talk is punishable,
Sweetheart, and there are warrants against women too.
100 CLÉANTE. Let's stop all this; Sir, we've had enough.
Just give us that paper and leave us. [*He takes the
paper from* LOYAL *and pushes him back toward the
door.*]

MONSIEUR LOYAL. Good-by until I see you again.
May Heaven keep all of you happy.

ORGON. [*As* LOYAL *goes out*] May it confound you
105 and him that sent you.

## SCENE V

ORGON, CLÉANTE, MARIANE, ELMIRE, MADAME PER-
NELLE, DORINE, DAMIS

ORGON. So! Mother, you see whether I was right
or not, and you may judge the rest by the summons.

*He hands the paper to* MADAME PERNELLE.] Do you understand his treachery now?

MADAM PERNELLE. I am stupefied and amazed. 5

DORINE. You complain without cause and blame him wrongfully, and this only confirms his pious intentions. His virtue reaches its highest point in the love of his neighbor. He knows that riches often make men corrupt, and out of pure charity he will remove anything 10 that may stand in the way of your salvation.

ORGON. You always have to be told to be quiet.

CLÉANTE. Let us consider what is to be done.

ELMIRE. Go and let everyone know of the audacity of the ungrateful rogue. This conduct destroys the 15 validity of the deed, and his disloyalty will appear too black for him to gain the success he imagines. [*The side door opens and all turn toward it.*]

## SCENE VI

### VALÈRE *and the rest*

VALÈRE. [*Entering quickly and going straight up to* ORGON] I am sorry, Sir, to bring you bad news, but I am forced to do so by the pressing danger. A dear friend of mine, who knows my concern for you, has violated the secrecy of state affairs and has just sent me a warning which forces you to flee at once. The 5 cheat who was able to deceive you for so long a time denounced you to the King about an hour ago and, among his other accusations, put into the King's hands the private papers of a criminal against the state; and he says that you, in defiance of a subject's duty, have 10 kept their dangerous secret. I do not know the details of the charges against you, but a warrant has been issued for your arrest, and the better to execute it, he himself is empowered to accompany the arresting officer. 15

CLÉANTE. Thus are his pretentions armed and by

this means the traitor seeks to make himself master of your property.

ORGON. I do confess, the man is an abominable
20 creature.

VALÈRE. The least delay may be fatal to you. My coach is at the door to carry you away, and I have here a thousand gold pieces for you. Let us lose no time. You are in terrible danger, and flight is the best
25 defense. [MARIANE *moves toward* VALÈRE.] I'll take you to a safe hiding place and will stay with you till the end of your flight. [VALÈRE *turns and takes* MARIANE *by the hands.*]

ORGON. Ah! What I do not owe to your kind concern! [*Moving toward the door*] I must thank you for
30 it all another time, and I beg Heaven to favor me so that I may someday acknowledge this generous service. Farewell, take care, all of you . . . [*All move toward the door as* ORGON *is about to go out.*]

CLÉANTE. Go quickly, Brother; we'll take care of all that's necessary. [*Just as* ORGON *reaches for the door, it opens and* TARTUFFE *enters followed by a police officer. The others all move back toward the center of the room.*]

SCENE VII

THE POLICE OFFICER, TARTUFFE, VALÈRE, ORGON, ELMIRE, MARIANE, ETC.

TARTUFFE. Softly, Sir, softly; do not run so fast. You need not go very far to find your lodging, for you are now the King's prisoner.

ORGON. [*Attempting to advance on* TARTUFFE *but held back by* CLÉANTE *and* ELMIRE] Traitor! You re-
5 served this stroke for the last. This is the blow, scoundrel, by which you finish me off, and this crowns all your viciousness. [*The officer moves to the center of the room.* TARTUFFE *is to his left; all the others are to his right.*]

TARTUFFE. Your abuses cannot provoke me, and I have learned to bear anything for the sake of Heaven.

CLÉANTE. Great moderation indeed! 10

DAMIS. How impudently the rogue plays with Heaven.

TARTUFFE. All your passion cannot move me. I think of nothing else but my duty.

MARIANE. You may indeed claim great glory from 15 this. These acts are very honorable in you.

TARTUFFE. An act cannot but be glorious when it comes from the power that sends me here.

ORGON. [Advancing toward TARTUFFE but still held back by the others] But do you remember, ungrateful wretch, that my charitable hand raised you from a 20 miserable condition.

TARTUFFE. Yes, I know what aid I have received from it, but the welfare of my Prince is my chief concern. [Turning toward the officer] The righteous force of this sacred duty stifles in my heart all other claims 25 and, for the sake of such powerful chains, I would sacrifice my friends, my wife, my family, and myself as well.

ELMIRE. [After a brief silence] The hypocrite!

DORINE. How treacherously he shields himself with 30 all that is sacred.

CLÉANTE. [To TARTUFFE] But if that concern which moves you and with which you adorn yourself be as honest as you say it is, why did it not appear until he surprised you in pursuit of his wife, and why did you 35 not think of denouncing him until his honor obliged him to turn you out? I say nothing of the gift of all his property, which might have turned you away from your plan, but, since you treat him like a criminal now, why were you willing to take anything from him be- 40 fore?

TARTUFFE. [Motioning to the officer] Relieve me of this noise, Sir, and be good enough, if you please, to execute your order. [TARTUFFE sits down in an arm *chair and looks around at the furniture, beaming.*]

45 POLICE OFFICER. Yes, I delay too long indeed. [*He crosses toward* ORGON, *then, while speaking, sharply turns and goes up to* TARTUFFEE, *and seizes him.*] You have just now most properly invited me to carry it out, and in order to do so, follow me at once to the prison you are to have for your lodging.

TARTUFFE. Who? I, Sir?

50 POLICE OFFICER. Yes, you.

TARTUFFE. Why to prison?

POLICE OFFICER. [*Pulling* TARTUFFE *out of the chair*] It is not to you that I'll give the explanation for it. [*To* ORGON] Calm yourself, Sir, after such a close call. We live under a Prince who is an enemy to fraud, a Prince 55 whose eyes penetrate to the heart and whom all the craft of hypocrites cannot deceive. His great soul is provided with a keen sense of discrimination, and always sees things in their true light. He is never taken in, and his firm reason falls into no excesses. He gives 60 to devout men an immortal glory, but he displays this piety without blindness, and his love for the truly pious does not shut his heart to the horror which hypocrites inspire. [*Pointing to* TARTUFFE] This man was not able to surprise him, for he guards himself 65 from even more cunning snares. At once his keen vision perceived all the villainy his heart conceals. Coming to accuse you, he betrayed himself, and, by a master-stroke of justice, was revealed to the Prince as a well-known cheat who had already been de-70 nounced under another name. His life is a long series of black deeds upon which volumes could be written. In a word, this monarch detested his mean ingratitude and his disloyalty to you. He has added this to his other crimes, and allowed me to be brought here by 75 him only to see his impudence go to the limit and to make him give you full satisfaction. Yes, he wills that I strip the traitor of all the papers he claims to own, and give them to you. [*He takes a bundle of papers*

*from* TARTUFFE'S *pocket.*] By his sovereign power he
breaks the obligation of the deed which made him 80
a gift of all your possessions, and pardons you for the
secret offense in which the flight of a friend involved
you. And this is his reward for the fidelity you have
previously displayed in support of his rights, to let
you know that when it is least expected, he knows how 85
to reward a good action [*He hands the papers to*
ORGON.], that merit, with him, is never unrecognized,
that he remembers the good far better than the evil.

DORINE. Heaven be praised!

MADAME PERNELLE. Now I can breathe.                    90

ELMIRE. A wonderful outcome!

MARIANE. Who could have imagined it?

ORGON. [*Rushing toward* TARTUFFE] Well now, here
you are, traitor, . . .

CLÉANTE. [*Restraining* ORGON.] Ah, Brother, hold, 95
and do not descend to indignities. [*The officer pushes*
TARTUFFE *out the door and closes it behind him.*]
Leave a miserable wretch to his fate and do not add
to his remorse. Rather wish that his heart may now
make a happy return to the bosom of virtue, that he
may reform his life by detesting his vice, and may 100
that great Prince soften the rigors of justice while
you go and on your knees, render to his goodness
what such generosity requires.

ORGON. Yes, that is well said. Let us throw ourselves joyfully at his feet, to show our gratitude for 105
the goodness he bestows on us. Then, when we have
performed this first duty, let us provide for the due
rights of another [*He takes* MARIANE *by one hand
and* VALÈRE *by the other.*], and let a happy marriage
crown in Valère the devotion of a noble and sincere 110
lover. [*The curtain falls.*]

# BIBLIOGRAPHY

THERE ARE SEVERAL excellent modern editions of Molière's complete works. The present text follows that
of Molière: *Œuvres Complètes* (Paris, Société Les
Belles Lettres, 1935-52; *Texte établi et présenté par
René Bray*). *Le Tartuffe* is found in Volume V, pp.
199-317. The student will find of special importance
the edition of *Le Tartuffe* in the collection of Molière's
complete works published in the series, "Les Grands
Ecrivains de la France" (Volume IV, pp. 269-566),
edited by Eugène Despois and Paul Mesnard (Paris,
1878). The school editions of *Le Tartuffe* prepared by
Pierre Clarac, "Classiques Larousse" (Paris, 1933) and
H. Ashton, "Blackwell's French Texts" (Oxford, 1957),
contain valuable explanatory material. Also of special
interest is the acting edition of *Le Tartuffe* prepared
by Fernand Ledoux, "Collection 'Mises en scène'"
(Paris, 1953).

Indispensable background material will be found
in Gustave Michaut, *Les Luttes de Molière* (Paris,
1925). Perhaps the best general study of the playwright is René Bray, *Molière, Homme du Théâtre*
(Paris, 1954). An excellent survey of the theatrical
background is provided by Henry Carrington Lan-
caster, *A History of French Dramatic Literature in the
Seventeenth Century, Part V: Recapitulation, 1610-
1700* (Baltimore, 1942). Among the most valuable
critical studies in English are Arthur Tilley, *Molière*
(Cambridge, 1921), John Palmer, *Molière* (New
York, 1930), and W. G. Moore, *Molière* (Oxford,
1949).